Practical Evaluation Guide

Tools for Museums and
Other Informal Educational Settings

ABOUT THE SERIES

The American Association for State and Local History Book Series publishes technical and professional information for those who practice and support history, and addresses issues critical to the field of state and local history. To submit a proposal or manuscript to the series, please request proposal guidelines from AASLH headquarters: AASLH Book Series, 1717 Church St., Nashville, Tennessee 37203. Telephone: (615) 320-3203. Fax: (615) 327-9013. Web site: www.aaslh.org.

ABOUT THE ORGANIZATION

The American Association for State and Local History (AASLH) is a nonprofit educational organization dedicated to advancing knowledge, understanding, and appreciation of local history in the United States and Canada. In addition to sponsorship of this book series, the Association publishes the periodical *History News*, a newsletter, technical leaflets and reports, and other materials; confers prizes and awards in recognition of outstanding achievement in the field; and supports a broad education program and other activities designed to help members work more effectively. To join the organization, contact: Membership Director, AASLH, 1717 Church St., Nashville, Tennessee 37203.

Practical Evaluation Guide

Tools for Museums and
Other Informal Educational Settings

Judy Diamond

ALTAMIRA
PRESS

A Division of
ROWMAN & LITTLEFIELD PUBLISHERS, INC.
Walnut Creek • Lanham • New York • Oxford

ALTAMIRA PRESS
A Division of Rowman & Littlefield Publishers, Inc.
1630 North Main Street, #367
Walnut Creek, CA 94596
www.altamirapress.com

Rowman & Littlefield Publishers, Inc.
4720 Boston Way
Lanham, MD 20706

12 Hid's Copse Road
Cumnor Hill, Oxford OX2 9JJ, England

Copyright © 1999 by AltaMira Press
Editorial Management: Pamela Lucas
Production Management and Services: David Featherstone
Cover Design: Joanna Ebenstein

British Library Cataloguing in Publication Information Available

Library of Congress Cataloging-in-Publication Data

Diamond, Judy.
    Practical evaluation guide : tools for museums and other informal educational
settings / Judy Diamond.
        p. cm. – (American Association for State and Local History book series)
    Includes bibliographical references and index.
    ISBN 0-7619-8939-0 (cloth)
    ISBN 0-7619-8940-4 (pbk.)
    1. Museum exhibits—Evaluation. 2. Museums—Educational aspects. 3. Non-formal
education. I. Title. II. Series.
    AM151 .D5 1999
    069'.5-dc21   98-14238
                                                                                      CIP

Printed in the United States of America

♾™ The paper used in this publication meets the minimum requirements of American
National Standard for Information Sciences—Permanence of Paper for Printed Library
Materials, ANSI/NISO Z39.48–1992.

To Benjamin and Rachel, for all that they teach me.

Contents

Illustrations

Tables

Preface and Acknowledgments

Most of the theories on how people learn are derived from research conducted in laboratories or schools. It is as if researchers have assumed that our experiences in other contexts have little consequence for our knowledge about human thinking and learning. Recently, however, this bias has begun to change, and increasing numbers of learning studies are being done in out-of-school, or informal, settings. The term *informal learning* refers to the kinds of learning people encounter as they go about their life outside formal educational settings. These experiences may occur at home, on street corners or playgrounds, while traveling, or while visiting institutions such as museums, zoos, aquaria, botanical gardens, and parks. Informal educational institutions offer people opportunities for learning that are as much entertainment as study.

Each year, over half a billion people visit museums, and these institutions spend more than $4 billion in federal, state, and private funds on their public and research programs (American Association of Museums 1994). Museums, zoos, gardens, and parks have all begun to ask how effective they are at meeting the needs of their audiences. Are people learning from, or even enjoying, their programs? Are they meeting the needs of specialized visitors? Are the dollars spent on exhibits and programs attracting bigger and more diverse audiences?

Visitor evaluation is a means of answering questions about the effectiveness of exhibits and programs, and it provides insight into how people learn in informal educational settings. From the occasional study in the 1920s and 1930s, visitor evaluation has grown into a major professional and research field. Visitor evaluation is now mandated by a number of federal agencies and private foundations as a condition for funding exhibits and programs.

This book gives step-by-step instructions on how to design, implement, and present an evaluation study, and it presents guidelines for studying the experiences of visitors in informal educational settings. Chapter one describes how to write an evaluation proposal and chose an evaluator. Chapter two presents the processes involved in informal learning and how these differ from the formal education found in schools. Chapter three recommends how to select subjects for an evaluation study to ensure a fair sample of the larger population; it also addresses how to protect the right of subjects to be fully informed about the nature of the research. Chapter four describes how to design and conduct an observational study in an informal educational setting. Chapter five presents ways to use interviews and written questionnaires as a means of gathering information. Chapter six explores the different tools that can measure informal learning directly, and chapter seven discusses how to present and analyze both qualitative and quantitative data. Finally, chapter eight describes how to present the results of an evaluation study in a clear and accessible format.

This book developed from many years of practical experience conducting evaluation studies in museums, primarily in science and natural history museums. During those years, I was fortunate enough to be part of the expanding movement in informal learning research. One center for this movement was an interdisciplinary graduate group located at the University of California at Berkeley. This group, called SESAME, brought together students from the sciences who had strong interests in educational questions relating to their disciplines. Students came into the group with backgrounds in biology, physics, mathematics, and computer science, and they conducted research in cognitive psychology, artificial intelligence, and informal learning. Many of the students interested in informal learning, including me, developed close ties to two innovative institutions in the San Francisco Bay Area—the Exploratorium and the Lawrence Hall of Science.

This book fills a niche in the ecology of museum-evaluation reference materials. There are several excellent books that provide overviews of what we now know about informal learning, and there are a number of books on specific types of evaluation methods or on theoretical approaches to museum evaluation. This book, however, is the first comprehensive guide to the methods used in informal evaluation, including both qualitative and quantitative approaches. It is designed as a practical introduction to the research tools of informal evaluation, in whatever context one might work. Many of the examples from this book are from science and natural history museums because those are where the author has spent many of the past twenty years conducting evaluation studies. The methods presented here have been written for, and will be useful for, any kind of informal institution, including those with a focus on art, history, or social issues.

There are many people who helped to make this book possible. Among the SESAME Group at the University of California at Berkeley, I wish to thank Sam Taylor, Mark St. John, Sherman Rosenfeld, John Falk, Jeff Gottfried, and especially Mac Laetsch. At the Exploratorium, I thank Rob Semper, Sally Duensing, Darlene Librero, Lynn Rankin, and the late Frank Oppenheimer, who always reminded me of the boundaries to evaluation studies, insisting that "You can't evaluate the stars."

I also thank Elsa Feher for many years of intriguing conversations and Mike Templeton for inspiration early in my career. Many thanks also go to Bonnie Van Dorn and Wendy Pollock, of the Association of Science and Technology Centers, and to Barbara Butler, of the Informal Science Education Program at the National Science Foundation, for their tireless efforts to further an understanding of informal learning. I wish to acknowledge the many students who have worked with me on evaluation and museum research projects, and who later conducted such projects themselves, developing their own innovative approaches. In particular, I would like to thank Dana Twersky, Cybele Londoño, and Anita Smith. I would like to give special appreciation to Peter Dow, Bonnie Sachetello-Sawyer, and one anonymous reviewer for their very helpful comments on an early draft of this manuscript. Finally, I thank Alan B. Bond for years of continuous support and inspiration.

Chapter 1

Planning an Evaluation Project

You want to study the visitors at your museum, zoo, botanical garden, or other informal educational institution, but where do you begin? You may want to know how well your new exhibit or program works. What does it communicate to visitors? How can you make improvements? What do you need to know about your audience? What are your visitors learning?

These questions can be answered by conducting evaluation studies at your institution. There is no single recipe for evaluations; each study should be designed to meet the specific needs of the institution or program being studied. There are, however, many different evaluation research methods to choose from.

Evaluation methods are tools that perform the function of gathering information. You probably would not try to cook a dinner using only one pot, and similarly you shouldn't think that one tool is sufficient to complete an evaluation study. According to Mark St. John,

> Different evaluation methods (experiments, case
> studies, surveys . . .) can be seen to be like the
> carpenter's hammer and saw—they are the evaluator's
> tools. Evaluators would do well to think of themselves
> as artists and craftsmen, and take pride in learning to
> use a wide range of tools skillfully. As carpenters do,
> evaluators can learn to eye a situation and know

instinctively which tools will work. As their skill
increases, evaluators can learn how to extend the
range of use of their tools, and even how to combine
their uses in innovative ways to accomplish more
difficult tasks. (1987b:2–3)

There are many kinds of evaluation studies, but most
can be identified as one of three types—front-end, formative, and summative. Front-end evaluation provides background information for future program planning. It can
tell about visitors' prior knowledge and experience, their
styles of learning, and their expectations regarding the institution. Front-end evaluation usually involves surveys or
interviews, but it can also include other methods for assessing information about visitors, such as observations of
typical behavior patterns and measurements of learning
styles. The primary goal of front-end evaluation is to learn
about the audience before a program or exhibit has been
designed in order to predict how visitors will respond
once the project has been developed. Essentially, front-
end evaluation identifies information about visitors that
can be incorporated into project or program design. This
information can help assure that the final product will meet
visitor needs and project goals.

Formative evaluation provides information about how
a program or exhibit can be improved. It occurs while a
project is under development. The evaluator measures visitor responses to models, plans, or prototypes of the program or exhibit. A prototype is a working version, usually
of an interactive exhibit. It should closely resemble the final product, although it may be constructed more roughly.
The more realistic the model or prototype, the more likely
it is that visitor reactions in the formative stage will anticipate reactions to the final product. Information from formative evaluation is used to make changes that improve
the design of a program or exhibit.

Summative evaluation tells about the impact of a project after it is completed. It is conducted after an exhibit has opened to the public or after a program has been presented. Summative evaluation can be as simple as a head count of how many people participated in the program, or it may be as complex as a study of what visitors learned. Generally, the results of a summative evaluation will be used to improve future activities through an understanding of existing programs.

The first step in an evaluation is to decide the topic and scope of the study. The following questions serve as a guide:

- What is the purpose of the study? Will your study be used to provide information for planning (front-end), information for improvements (formative), or information on the overall impact of a program (summative)?

- Who is it for? Is your study being conducted for an internal audience or an external audience? Is it for the institution's decision-makers, program staff, outside funders, other researchers, or all of the above? To whom will you present your report? The immediate audience for your study is often referred to as the "client." Typically, an internal client for informal education evaluation studies may be an administrator, educator, designer, or curator, or sometimes members of the board of trustees or community advisory board. An external client may be a program officer at a funding agency, a design consultant, or a public agency representative to whom the institution is accountable.

- What do you hope to produce as a result of your study? What will your final report look like? Do you plan to publish it in a museum, zoo, or education journal? Will you want a summary report as well as a detailed report? Will the findings be presented orally?

- Who will undertake the study? Will you use an internal evaluation (a staff member of the institution being studied) or an external evaluator (an unaffiliated evaluation professional)?

Evaluating the Evaluator

Evaluation of an informal setting can be conducted by an institution's own staff, by outside professional evaluators, or by staff working together with outside experts. Each alternative has its own advantages and disadvantages. When staff from an institution choose to evaluate a program or exhibit, they take on the responsibility to be objective and neutral, without regard to their relationship to the project. The advantages of internal or staff evaluators are many. Staff may already know the relevant issues without time-consuming background research. They may know who the most useful people are to get insight from, including former employees and others with important, but minimal contacts with the institution. Because they are on-site, staff evaluators may be more convenient for other staff to talk to, and the study can be made more flexible for the institution. They may be much less expensive since there are no travel expenses and no hourly or daily consulting rates. Finally, staff evaluators are in the position to apply experience from one study to subsequent ones.

The disadvantages of staff evaluators are that they may be less objective than professional evaluators, particularly if they feel strongly invested in the project or institution; they also may be less skillful. Sometimes, even when their skill levels are equivalent to those of outside evaluators, others in the institution may not accord staff evaluators the same credibility.

There are many professional outside evaluators who specialize in the evaluation of informal educational programs or institutions. Some of these individuals are on the faculty of universities, while others have private consulting groups. The American Association of Museums (AAM) supports a Committee on Audience Research and Evaluation that provides the names of museum evaluators to interested parties. The advantages of using outside evaluators are that they generally have highly developed skills in research and evaluation and that they may have a great deal of experience conducting similar studies. In addition, sometimes staff members feel that because outsiders have no personal investment in the project, they are easier to talk to.

The disadvantages of outside evaluators are that they sometimes cannot give the amount of time needed, they can be much more expensive, and they generally cannot provide day-to-day guidance in implementing the evaluation results.

The best of all worlds may be a staff evaluator who collaborates with an outside professional. When that professional can be found in a local university or consulting group, the possibility for long-term collaborative relationships becomes feasible. These professionals may be found in a department of educational psychology, sociology, or psychology. It helps greatly for them to have some museum experience, and if they are paired with a knowledgeable staff evaluator, one can maximize the advantages of on-site experience with the objectivity of an outsider.

The AAM Committee on Audience Research and Evaluation recommends that the following basic competencies should be required for professional practice (Shettel 1993: 65–66):

- Evaluators should have knowledge of the relevant literature in visitor studies and the associated social sciences.

- They should have a general understanding of the practices and procedures of museum operations.

- They need a working knowledge of social science research design and the related methodological and analytical skills.

- They should be skilled in effective communication and information-gathering techniques.

- They should be committed to the dissemination of evaluation studies through publication in journals, presentation at national meetings, and other activities that further the development of the field of visitor research and evaluation.

The Evaluation Proposal

After deciding the overall scope of your evaluation study, the next step is to prepare a brief proposal that will give colleagues a summary of what you plan to accomplish. The proposal should be readable and concise, and it should not overstate the scope of the study. Such a document is a very useful way of communicating with other staff, since it gives them the opportunity to learn about the study plan and provide necessary feedback. The following outline serves as a guide for an evaluation study proposal:

- *Background*: In one to two pages, describe the institution, project, or exhibition that you will be evaluating, and include simple drawings or photographs if they are available. State the overall purpose and timeline of the evaluation study.

- *Evaluation project objectives*: Specifically, what do you hope to accomplish during your evaluation study?

What are four to six activities that you will undertake with your study? At least one of these objectives should include a statement of how you will involve the institution's staff. You might indicate, for example, that you will include an exhibits or education committee in a total of three planning meetings and, at the end of the study, lead a discussion of the findings with members of that committee. A second objective might refer to the fact that you plan to design site-specific evaluation instruments that could be used by the institution's staff in the future. Other objectives should state the purpose of the study in terms of measurable outcomes. For example, you might say you will characterize the zoo or museum audience over the past three years based on gender, ethnicity, socioeconomic background, and level of education. Mention specifically any parts of the program or exhibit that you do not plan to evaluate.

- *Proposed timeline*: State when the evaluation study will begin, when data will be collected and analyzed, and when the final report will be completed. Be sure you are realistic in your time commitments. Consider weekly or seasonal variations in visitor use when you estimate how long it will take to collect the data. Remember that it can take much longer to analyze data than to collect it.

- *Evaluation methods*: Outline the design of your study in a couple of paragraphs, then give some idea of the methods that you will use to carry it out. For example, you might indicate that you would conduct observations and interviews of a sample of fifty typical museum visitors while they are using an exhibit prototype. Or you may state that you will conduct phone interviews with 150 program participants. Specify whether you plan to use qualitative findings that summarize subjects' responses and interpretations in narrative form as well as quantitative data with statistical analysis to summarize the results.

- *Products*: A useful product of your study is often a brief summary report, backed up by a longer background report. Most of the people who read your report will only be interested in the summary. Sometimes it is helpful to provide a debriefing session for interested staff as well.

After you have completed your evaluation proposal, share it with your client or staff, and encourage them to give you feedback on its content. Pay close attention to the responses of the staff. They sometimes have spent years watching and interacting with visitors, and their insights can help to assure that your study is relevant to the needs and expectations of the institution. Listen carefully to what the staff emphasize about the institution's overall function, and notice what different constituencies exist within the institution. Every institution has a cultural climate that will influence the response to your evaluation and, ultimately, its usefulness. The reactions to the evaluation proposal will begin to give you an indication of the institutional climate and the nature of people's expectations.

Quantitative and Qualitative Evaluation Methods

Evaluation studies in informal settings draw on research methods from a variety of disciplines in the social and biological sciences. One primary distinction in these research approaches is between quantitative and qualitative methods.

Quantitative methods attempt to classify diverse opinions or behaviors into established categories. Quantitative studies are designed to look for numerical patterns in data, summarizing the reactions of many people to a limited set of variables. Quantitative methods often make comparisons between categories of data by using statistical tests to establish the nature of the relationships among variables. They may include experiments, tests, observations, surveys, or other means of comparing the responses or behavior of different groups. A primary advantage of quantitative methods is that they provide findings that can be generalized to larger populations.

Qualitative methods, on the other hand, emphasize depth of understanding over the generalizability of the data. Qualitative methods allow the evaluator to examine individual cases or events in depth and detail. These methods may emphasize overall trends, but they may also seek out exceptions, particularly how special cases differ from the mainstream. Qualitative methods utilize direct quotations, open-ended narrative, detailed reporting of events, and behavioral observation. Qualitative studies can be especially helpful when you are just starting to examine a problem, and also whenever the important issues are not yet clear. They are also very effective as a way of understanding complex phenomena that cannot be easily summarized into discrete categories.

Quantitative and qualitative methods are best used in tandem, so that the strengths of each approach can be put to advantage. A single evaluation study may use qualitative methods to generate ideas, categories, and questions, while at the same time it uses quantitative methods to verify those results for a larger population. Together, the two approaches combine insight, depth, and an appreciation for differences with consistency, predictability, and the ability to generalize broadly.

Regardless of which research methods are used, there are some general guidelines on how to approach an informal evaluation study. Mark St. John (1987a:8) summarizes some of the ways that, as an evaluator, you can learn the most from subjects:

- Begin by not knowing what to do. Try not to restrict the evaluation to a predetermined task or method. Keep an open mind at the beginning.

- Begin with what is happening. Study the program as it is, and don't be blinded by someone else's concerns. Ground yourself in a personal knowledge of the program.

- Work from the general to the specific. Let your vision mature slowly and change along the way.

- Use both analytic and integrative modes of thinking. Analysis is needed to discover and separate out the important dimensions of the scene, while an integrated vision is required to create an encompassing vision of the evaluation in its entirety. Let these two modes of thought interact.

- Formulate general questions to guide the evaluation. Questions such as "How can we understand what is happening in this program?" or "What are the barriers to this program's effectiveness?" can begin to lead you to more specific analysis.

- Use evaluation methods flexibly. Make creative use of the wide range of methods that are available to you.

- Monitor, recycle, and rethink. Assume your plan is going to evolve and change—then the final evaluation is more likely to meet the institution's needs.

Chapter 2

Informal Learning

Either directly or indirectly, most evaluation studies will touch on how people learn in informal settings. Learning in museums and similar institutions is called informal learning to differentiate it from the formal learning that occurs in school settings. Typically described as everything that school learning is not, informal learning has the following characteristics:

- It occurs voluntarily; no one is mandated to learn in a museum.

- It has no established sequence or curriculum.

- It can occur in a variety of settings, including institutions such as museums, zoos, botanical gardens, and aquaria. It may also occur at programs such as camps, fairs, festivals, and clubs, and at locations such as playgrounds, parks, homes, or even street corners.

- It is ubiquitous. It occurs in many places, at any time of the day, and at any time of one's life.

According to the Informal Science Education Program of the National Science Foundation, informal learning is voluntary and self-directed, life-long, and motivated mainly by intrinsic interests, curiosity, exploration, manipulation, fantasy, task completion, and social interaction. Informal learning can be linear or non-linear and often is self-paced and visual- or object-oriented. It provides an experiential base and motivation for further activity and learning. The outcomes of an informal learning experience in science, mathematics, and technology include a better understanding of concepts, topics, processes, and thinking in scientific and technical disciplines, as well as increased knowledge about career opportunities in these fields. (1998:7)

Frank Oppenheimer and K. C. Cole point out that informal learning generally does not confer degrees or levels of accomplishment; there are no prerequisites, you cannot graduate, and you cannot fail.

Museums are a vast resource of props for discovery; they can relieve any of the tensions which make learning in school ineffective or even painful. No one ever "fails" in a museum. One museum is not a prerequisite for the next. (1974:8)

Informal learning is frequently an intensely social experience occurring in the context of family or peers. It is characterized by social facilitation, in which people are unconsciously influenced to imitate or follow others, resulting in new learning experiences. Through social facilitation, adults in museums influence children to spend more time at the exhibits, thereby giving them the opportunity for more in-depth experiences (Diamond et al. 1988). Informal learning also involves observational learning, wherein people learn by watching the behavior of others. In museums, observational learning is a primary mechanism by which visitors learn how to operate interactive exhibits (Diamond 1980, Hilke 1989). Informal learning also involves teaching, through which group members direct and reinforce each other's attention and actions (Hilke 1989, Hilke and Balling 1985). Diamond (1980) and Dierking (1987) showed that, among families visiting museums, teaching is likely to be reciprocal, with children as likely to teach adults as vice-versa.

A large element of informal learning involves play, which can be either solitary or social. In zoos, parks, and many museums, play is not only tolerated, but also often encouraged. People who play at museum exhibits often spend more time at them, manipulating them in often unexpected ways (Diamond 1986, 1996). The result is that play at exhibits often leads to a more thorough knowledge of exhibit phenomena. Play can also be part of the informal teaching process: At the Exploratorium in San Francisco, the teenage Explainers use play not only as a means of mass entertainment, but also as a way of demonstrating exhibit operations to the public (Diamond et al. 1987).

According to Frank Oppenheimer, the founding director of the Exploratorium, play and exploration become the means for experiencing the informal environment in a personal and individualized way:

> A large part of the play of children involves using
> common physical and cultural components of society
> in a context that is divorced from its primary purpose.
> It is through such inventive and repetitive play that
> they learn to feel at home with the world. In this
> fashion our exhibits are also playful. . . . In exhibits
> that are obviously intended for play, exhibits that
> themselves use props divorced from their original
> context, all manner of lovely things are discoverable,
> even by the people who invent them. (1972:982)

Informal learning may emphasize different thinking processes than those that are found among children in schools. According to Don Norman (1982), understanding is the process of putting materials to be learned into existing frameworks of knowledge that guide their retrieval. In informal learning, however, the appropriate mental frameworks may not be established beforehand, and this requires a more indirect and eclectic assembly of knowledge structures. Oppenheimer likens the informal learning process to sightseeing:

> The individual sights combine to form patterns, which constitute a simple form of understanding. The process continues beyond this stage as groups of seemingly disparate patterns then coalesce to form the patterns that provide the deepest insights about nature. We are exploring various forms of museum teaching and learning at the Exploratorium, but our effort would be worthwhile even if it did no more than provide some good sightseeing. (1972:979)

To Elsa Feher, learning at interactive exhibits is a process that involves four levels of understanding, each of which is a precursor to the next level. At the first level, experiencing, the visitor experiences phenomena of which he or she was previously unaware or incompletely aware. This experience is perceptual and sensory, driven by emotional qualities more than purely cognitive ones. In the second level, exploring, the user discovers new features of the phenomena by manipulating the exhibit. The third level, explaining, is conceptual; it deals most directly with cognitive issues. The fourth and final level, expanding, involves the generalization of ideas through the involvement of related exhibits. One exhibit by itself cannot carry the whole conceptual message, so multiple exhibits on one topic are necessary to extend the user's worldview.

Cognitive changes occur in the museum as visitors compare the results of their experimentation with the results they expected. If the results are different from what was expected, the visitors are surprised. According to Feher, one kind of surprise arises when the difference between actual occurrence and expectations can be explained within the visitor's existing mental framework. Without abrupt cognitive discontinuities, the visitor can assimilate the new result:

> The other kind of surprise occurs when the difference between the phenomenon observed and the visitor's expectation cannot be explained within an existing mental framework. That is, if the exhibit is truly confrontational, we expect that the user of the exhibit will need to shift his or her mental framework and that cognitive change will occur. In our work this happened with learners who were in a transitional stage, almost ready to take the conceptual jump. (1990:47)

One reason that informal knowledge differs from school-based knowledge is that the goals are different. According to Fred Reif and Jill Larkin, the goals in the school environment are largely focused on satisfying criteria specified by teachers, textbooks, examinations, and other sources of accepted authority. Informal knowledge emphasizes the experiences of everyday life.

> Knowledge in everyday life is ordinarily not deliberately sought, but spontaneously acquired through interaction with the world and other people. Thus people sometimes say that they understand something merely because they have experience with it. They may also say that they understand aspects of the world if they can explain or predict them sufficiently well so that they can make sense of them and interact with them satisfactorily. Past experience, and local knowledge about specific contexts, are generally quite adequate for such commonly needed predictions and explanations. . . .

> There are no well-defined criteria of what constitutes understanding in everyday life. In particular, there are no requirements for inference chains based on well-specified premises and inference rules. Thus people may claim that they understand something because they can relate it, by reasonable arguments, to common sense or other familiar knowledge. Similarly, understanding may be demonstrated by explanations that merely identify a perceived causative agent or note some connections among relevant features. (1991:741)

Children as well as adults solve everyday problems by relying on accumulated knowledge and by using this knowledge to make relatively short inferences in particular contexts. These methods depend heavily on perceptual processes, pattern recognition, and qualitative reasoning. As Reif and Larkin point out, these methods are usually sufficient to attain everyday goals with adequate precision and consistency. Problem-solving in everyday informal environments may not rely at all on the rule-based reasoning that is characteristic of scientific problem-solving.

The study of informal learning requires an appreciation for its subtlety. Since it is not rule-based or driven by external demands such as tests, informal learning is often implicit. Implicit learning occurs when we learn to respond appropriately without being able to state the rules that govern our behavior. In implicit learning, people may lack metaknowledge about their knowledge. According to Dienes and Berry (1977), people may believe they are guessing when in fact they are using unconscious rules, and they may not be able to describe how a task was performed.

Jeremy Roschelle has recently examined how a learner's prior learning shapes the way that she or he develops new understandings. A learner's prior knowledge can confound the best efforts to deliver ideas accurately, and there is widespread agreement that prior knowledge influences learn-

ing and that learners construct concepts from prior knowledge. Roschelle argues that learning proceeds primarily
from prior knowledge and only secondarily from the presented materials. Prior knowledge thus largely determines
what we learn from experience, and it can both interfere
with and facilitate learning. Roschelle calls this the "paradox of continuity." He suggests a few guidelines for designers of interactive experiences:

> First, designers should seek to refine prior knowledge,
> not attempt to replace learners' understanding with
> their own. Second, designers must anticipate a long-
> term learning process, of which the short-term
> experience will form an incremental part. Third,
> designers must remember that learning depends on
> social interaction; conversations shape the form and
> content of the concepts that learners construct. Only
> part of specialized knowledge can exist explicitly as
> information; the rest must come from engagement in
> the practice of discourse of the community. (1995:40)

These notions of learning have implications for what
you might expect to find in a museum or other informal
learning environment. Roschelle argues against an exces-
sive focus on knowledge. If you only measure the amount
of knowledge acquired by visitors, you are likely to miss
essential parts of the learning experience.

> Dramatic conceptual change is a slow, unpredictable,
> and difficult process. It is thus inappropriate to expect
> deep conceptual change to occur predictably, in a
> single or short series of visits. Conversely, when deep
> conceptual change does occur, it will almost certainly
> involve resources beyond the museum's control such
> as books, videos, science kits, classes, clubs, and so
> forth. Thus in assessing museum learning, we can
> neither overemphasize nor ignore prior knowledge.
> (1995:49)

The distinctions between informal and formal learning may sometimes blur. In fact, for every rule that defines informal learning there are also exceptions. Classes are taught in museums and zoos, and sometimes these may be mandated, structured, follow a curriculum, and result in grades. Increasingly, there are efforts to interweave the programs of informal learning institutions with those of schools (Hofstein and Rosenfeld 1996). Several museums, including the California Museum of Science and Industry in Los Angeles and the Buffalo Museum of Natural History, play major roles in operating accredited public schools whose students participate actively in both school and museum activities. There are now many different collaborations that combine elements of museum and school, zoo and school, or aquarium and school. For a typical example, the Folsom Children's Zoo in Lincoln, Nebraska, cooperates with the local public secondary school to offer a two-year "school in the zoo" curriculum as an alternative to the conventional high school program.

According to John Falk and Lynn Dierking (1992), informal learning has distinct advantages over its more organized counterpart. Informal learning prepares the individual for life-long learning. It teaches people that learning is a part of everyday life, that it requires initiative, and that everyone, regardless of background, is allowed to participate. Informal learning provides no immediate external rewards, but it reinforces learning for its own sake. Most of all, informal learning reminds us that learning can be fun, that it can be enjoyed as excitement, exploration, and play.

Chapter 3

Protecting and Selecting Subjects

Protecting Subjects' Rights

Researchers have a legal and ethical obligation to make sure that the rights of subjects are protected. This obligation is just as important when you are studying people on a playground or in a museum as when you bring them into an experimental laboratory. Because informal institutions are generally public environments, it is very easy to gather data about people without their being aware of what is occurring. Nevertheless, subjects should always be given sufficient knowledge of an evaluation or other research project to make an informed decision about whether or not they want to participate. Most projects in informal settings involve minimal risk and will not adversely affect the individuals' rights, but subjects still have a right to be well informed about the nature of the research and its possible consequences.

Guidelines for the protection of research subjects were first codified at the end of World War II during the war crime trials in Nuremberg. These guidelines, called the Nuremberg Code, were drafted as a set of standards for judging scientists who had conducted medical experiments on concentration camp prisoners. The code has served as a basis for subsequent efforts to create ethical guidelines for conducting research. In 1974, when the National Research Act was signed into law, a commission was created to identify the basic ethical principles that should underlie the conduct of all biomedical and behavioral research involving human subjects. The commission was further asked to develop guidelines that should be followed to ensure that such research is conducted in accordance with the principles. In 1979, the commission created the Belmont Report (Department of Health, Education, and Welfare 1979), which soon was adopted as federal policy.

Universities are now required to set up committees to oversee compliance with the Belmont Report and other federal guidelines for protecting the rights of research subjects. These are called human subjects committees or institutional review boards, and they review research plans of all university studies that involve human subjects. A central element of the review is the concept of informed consent, which describes how subjects are informed about all of the possible impacts of participating in a research project. Subjects must also fully understand their right not to participate in the research. Typically an investigator submits an overview of a research project, with specific details on how subjects will be informed about their rights. The committee or board then reviews the information and ultimately gives permission before the project can proceed.

Most informal educational institutions lack formal procedures for reviewing research or evaluation projects that use human visitors as subjects. Very few have any established process to ensure that their visitors are adequately protected, so informed consent becomes the obligation of the individual evaluator or investigator. See figures 1 and 2 for examples of consent forms.

 University of
Nebraska
Lincoln

University of Nebraska State Museum
Morrill Hall
P.O. Box 880338
Lincoln, NE 68588-0338
(402) 472-6302
FAX (402) 472-8899

Child Assent Form

Multimedia Exhibit on Paleontology

1. We are building a new museum exhibits hall about the Age of Dinosaurs. As part of that hall, we would like to build a computer-based exhibit that is fun to use and educational. We would like to invite you to help us develop that exhibit. You are eligible to take part because you have some experience with the University of Nebraska State Museum's programs.

2. Please talk this over with your parents before you decide whether or not to participate. Your parents will also be asked to give their permission for you to take part in this study.

3. If you have any questions at any time, please ask.

4. You will be asked to try out different versions of a computer-based exhibit on paleontology. We will want to know what you like and don't like about the exhibit, and how you think we should make it better.

5. We will watch you use the exhibit on various occasions, up to 12 different times. Sometimes you will be asked to use the exhibit by yourself, and sometimes with other kids.

6. Your participation with help us make this exhibit to be more fun and educational for kids.

You are making a decision whether or not to be in this study. Signing this form means that you have decided to participate and have read all that is on this form. You and your parents will be given a copy of this assent form to keep.

_____   _____
Signature of Subject   Date

_____   _____
Signature of Investigator   Date

Principal Investigator: Dr. Judy Diamond 472-6365.

Figure 1. Assent form sent to children who participated in the formative evaluation of a multimedia exhibit on the Age of Dinosaurs at the University of Nebraska State Museum.

 University of
Nebraska
Lincoln

MUSEUM STUDIES PROGRAM
307 Morrill Hall
Lincoln, NE 68588-0356
(402) 472-6365

Parental Informed Consent Form

You are invited to permit your child to participate in this research study at the University of
Nebraska State Museum. The following information is provided in order to help you make an
informed decision whether or not to allow your child to participate. If you have any
questions please do not hesitate to ask.

Your child is eligible to participate in this study because he or she is very familiar with the
activities and programs of the University of Nebraska State Museum. Your child has been
selected because we believe he or she may be able to give us useful feedback on the
development of some of our exhibits.

We are creating a new exhibit hall, entitled Mesozoic Monsters, Mammals, and Magnolias.
As part of this hall, we are developing a multimedia exhibit on paleontology. A multimedia
exhibit uses a computer and videodisc to enable visitors to have a participatory experience in
the Museum. We would observe your child using various versions of the exhibit, and we
would interview your child about what he or she likes and doesn't like about the exhibit, what
he and she learns from the exhibit, and how he or she would like to see it changed to be more
fun and interesting. There will be a maximum of 12 interview and observation sessions
conducted over the course of a year.

There are no known risks associated with this research. Any information obtained during this
study which could identify your child will be kept strictly confidential, unless you specifically
request that such information be released. The information obtained in this study may be
published in museum and/or science education journals or presented at museum and/or science
education meetings, but your child's identity will be kept strictly confidential.

_____ Parent's Initials

Your child's rights as a research subject have been explained to you. If you have any
additional questions concerning your child's rights, you may contact the University of
Nebraska Institutional Review Board (IRB) at 402-472-6965.

Figure 2. Consent form sent to parents of children who participated in the formative
evaluation of a multimedia exhibit on the Age of Dinosaurs at the University of Nebraska
State Museum. Parents are asked to give informed consent for their child's participation.

You are free to decide not to have your child participate in this study or to withdraw your child at any time without adversely affecting their or your relationship with the investigator, the University of Nebraska State Museum or the University of Nebraska. Your decision with not result in any loss of benefits to which your child is otherwise entitled.

DOCUMENTATION OF INFORMED CONSENT

YOU HAVE VOLUNTARILY MADE A DECISION WHETHER OR NOT TO ALLOW YOUR CHILD TO PARTICIPATE IN THIS RESEARCH STUDY. YOUR SIGNATURE CERTIFIES THAT YOU HAVE DECIDED TO ALLOW YOUR CHILD TO PARTICIPATE HAVING READ AND UNDERSTOOD THE INFORMATION PRESENTED. YOU WILL BE GIVEN A COPY OF THIS CONSENT FORM TO KEEP.

_____   _____

Signature of Parent   Date

IN MY JUDGEMENT THE PARENT/LEGAL GUARDIAN IS VOLUNTARILY AND KNOWINGLY GIVING INFORMED CONSENT AND POSSESSES THE LEGAL CAPACITY TO GIVE INFORMED CONSENT TO PARTICIPATE IN THIS RESEARCH STUDY.

_____   _____

Signature of Investigator   Date

IDENTIFICATION OF INVESTIGATORS:

Principal Investigator: Dr. Judy Diamond
                         (o) 402-472-6365

Figure 2, continued.

The legal standard of informed consent requires that prospective subjects be provided with the following information (University of Nebraska-Lincoln Institutional Review Board 1997:10):

- A general description of the research, including the purpose for which it is being performed, the duration for which the subject is expected to participate, why the participant was selected, age of the participants (under nineteen requires parental consent), a description of the procedures to be followed, where the research will take place, and the exact nature of any procedures that are experimental.

- An account of any reasonably foreseeable risks or discomforts to the subject.

- A description of any benefits to the participant or to others which may reasonably be expected from the research.

- A disclosure of appropriate alternative procedures or courses of treatment, if any, that might be advantageous to the participant.

- A commitment to maintenance of confidentiality in subject records and a description as to how confidentiality will be maintained.

- A statement of the subject's right to ask questions and to have those questions answered, and the name and phone number of people to contact for answers to any questions about the research. This includes questions about the rights of research subjects.

- A statement of whom to contact concerning questions about research participants' rights (a local university institutional review board, for example).

- A statement that participation is voluntary, that refusal to participate will involve no penalty or loss of benefits to which the subject is otherwise entitled, and that the subject may discontinue participation at any time without loss of benefits to which the subject is otherwise entitled.

If you think that participation in the study might involve more than minimal risk, you should include an explanation of any compensation that is offered as well as whether medical treatment is available should an injury occur, what that treatment consists of, and where further information may be obtained.

Some subjects require special protection because they may not be able to make informed decisions about their participation in the study. Special care must be taken to ensure the rights of children and other individuals who lack self-determination. This may include people subject to illness, disability, or other circumstances that may restrict freedom of choice.

One of the possible consequences of following ethical guidelines is that fully informing a subject about her participation in a research project may result in altering her behavior or opinions during the research. If the process of obtaining informed consent has been carefully conducted, however, the impact of knowing about the study is likely to be small. Nevertheless, if the researcher thinks that the research process itself has influenced the outcome of the study, it is important that this be considered when generalizations are made from the study results.

Most often, honesty and openness in the presentation of research will make the project appear less threatening. Sometimes subjects mistakenly believe that the purpose of the research is to make judgments about their performance, so it can be very reassuring if they know that the purpose is to make improvements in the institution or its programs.

How Many Subjects?

How many subjects should you include in your study? The sample size and the sampling method will have a major impact on the interpretation of your results. If your sample has been carefully selected, then what holds true for the sample is more likely to be correct for the entire population. Bias in sampling, or too small a sample, will skew the findings, so that information from the sample may not be true of the public at large.

The nature of your study questions will determine the sampling method. Small sample sizes are useful when the purpose of the research is to generate new ideas that may be followed up in more detail later. A focus group of fifteen to twenty subjects may be a very useful way of discovering problems and issues to pursue in later investigations. In one study, we used a group of seven children to give us feedback on the prototypes of a multimedia program. More subjects would not have been particularly helpful to us at that stage in our evaluation.

The sample size depends on the following:

- How much sampling error you are willing to tolerate.

- The size and variability of the population of interest.

- The smallest subgroup within the population for which estimates are needed.

There are various guidelines that can help you select the size of your subject sample:

- About five to ten subjects may be useful for exploratory evaluations that raise questions to be pursued later. Focus groups may comfortably include fifteen to twenty subjects. Qualitative studies may sample subjects from a variety of different subgroups in order to get as much variability as possible.

- About forty to sixty individuals are required in order to provide a pool large enough for most kinds of quantitative analysis.

- In quantitative studies, choose a sample that is large enough so that each cell in your analytical table contains at least five to ten subjects. First, create a dummy table with the subject groups listed in the left column and the analytical categories along the top (see table 1).

Table 1. Example of a table with a three-by-three design. If you have five samples in each cell and nine cells, then the total number of subjects needed is 45.

Grade	School A	School B	School C
K–2	5	5	5
3–5	5	5	5
6–8	5	5	5

Note in table 2 that, as a population gets larger, you eventually reach a point where the required sample changes only very little, or not at all. Thus, if you can accept a 10 percent sampling error, and the museum has a million visitors each year, it is reasonable to make generalizations on the basis of a random sample of ninety-six visitors. This is the same sample size that you would use if the museum had fifty thousand visitors or one hundred million visitors. It is more common to require a sampling error of 3 percent, and still there is only one more subject required for a population of one hundred million than for a population of one million. This is why pollsters, who generally require a 3 percent sampling error, can make generalizations about an entire country's population based on a sample of only a few thousand.

Table 2. The sample size needed for different sizes of populations. The sampling error is a measure of the potential error that occurs when researchers gather data from only a sample, instead of the entire population.

population size	+/- 3% sampling error	+/- 10% sampling error
100	92	49
500	341	81
1,000	516	88
5,000	880	94
10,000	964	95
50,000	1045	96
100,000	1056	96
1,000,000	1066	96
100,000,000	1067	96

Source: Adapted from Salant and Dillman (1994:55)

Selecting Subjects for Quantitative Studies

After establishing the sample size, the next step is to decide how to select the subjects. The method for selecting subjects can differ depending on whether you use quantitative or qualitative methods. This section discusses how to select subjects when using quantitative methods; in these studies, how you select the subjects will have a bearing on how broadly you can generalize your results to an overall population.

When you are studying a fairly small population (e.g., people who have taken classes at the museum), you may find that you are able to include all of the members as subjects. In this case you are not really sampling from the population, because you are able to include everybody that you are interested in studying. Most often, however, your population is too large to include every member in your study. In these cases, you have to sample a smaller group of subjects that will give you an indication of how the larger population will respond.

Two common methods for sampling are systematic and representational sampling. In systematic sampling, subjects are selected so that there are equivalent numbers from each group (table 3). Systematic sampling lends itself to some kinds of statistical analysis in which it is desirable to have an equal sample size in each category.

Table 3. An example of systematic sampling for gender and age. Half of the subjects in each age group are male and half are female. Half of the subjects of each gender are adults and half are children.

	Females	Males
Adults	20	20
Children	20	20

Sometimes you will want to select your subjects on the basis of how frequently individuals with specific demographic characteristics appear in the overall population. This is called representational sampling. Representational sampling determines sample sizes of each category in proportion to its frequency in the population of interest (table 4). If you are selecting your subjects by their ethnic group or age, you may want to select group members by how frequently they appear in the museum population. For example, if senior citizens make up 60 percent of your audience, children under twenty make up 20 percent, and nonsenior adults make up the other 20 percent, you may want to select your sample according to these percentages.

Whether you use systematic or representational sampling, you will need some method for choosing which individuals will be included. You will need some way of ensuring that any member of the population has an equal chance of being included in your sample. It is very important that you do not choose your subjects on the basis of some other, possibly biased criteria (e.g., subjects who look nonthreatening, who are well dressed, or who speak to you first). One practical method is to set up a system for alter-

Table 4. An example of representational sampling for ethnicity. If the larger population of your region consists of 30% Hispanic, 10% African American, 40% Caucasian, 10% Asian, 5% Pacific Islander, 4% Native American, and 1% other ethnic groups, and your total sample size is 200, this table shows what the representational sample would be.

	Hispanic	African American	Causacian	Asian	Pacific Islander	Native American	Other
Adults and Children	60	20	80	20	10	8	2

nating your choices: If you are sampling female and male adults, for example, you can choose the first female who walks in the door and ask her to participate. If she agrees, then you return to the door and approach the next male who walks in and ask him to participate. Some researchers advocate choosing the fifth subject from each category who appears at the designated selection location; this approach can be useful when there are large numbers of visitors entering at the same time.

The method of alternating choices is acceptable when the likelihood of each type of subject entering the building is about the same. However, when you want to sample systematically by age or ethnicity and some classes of subjects are relatively rare, you may have to wait days to complete your sampling. In such cases, it is best to be practical. If you are sampling systematically by age and only a few people in the age category over sixty come into your institution, then you may want to include nearly all of the people in this category, regardless of when they enter. When you write up your findings, you will need to consider how this might have biased your results and discuss the effect of that bias in your conclusions. In informal settings, where you are greatly limited in how much control you can exert over the environment, it is often necessary to be practical and opportunistic. This does not mean that you should ignore the rules of sampling. Rather, it implies that you should try to select your sample in the most unbiased way possible, then carefully consider any sources of bias that might result.

You can choose subjects in any number of ways:

- As they enter or exit the building or room.

- From membership lists, visitor sign-in books, museum classes, or clubs.

- From people walking near the museum or in other public places.

- From phone books.

If you want typical casual visitors as your subjects, then you probably want to select people who are entering or leaving the building, program, or exhibit. If you are study-ing only people that have a more intensive involvement in the institution, then you might want to use membership, class, or volunteer lists.

There is never a perfect time to choose your subjects. If you approach them as they enter the institution, they may be in a hurry, concerned that they may miss time with the exhibits or programs. If you approach them at the end of the visit, they may have already run out of time and need to get to their next activity. In either case, be sure to tell potential subjects right away how much of their time you will need, then be sure to end promptly on time. If you plan to interview adults with children, then either make the children the focus of the interview or provide super-vised activity for the children so the adult can focus atten-tion on your questions. It can be very useful to offer some-thing in exchange for your subject's time. The offer of a free pass to the facility, a free planetarium show, or a free poster or gift certificate at the museum store can be a use-ful way of motivating subjects who might not otherwise feel inclined to give you their time. For longer interviews, it is best to make initial contact with your subjects at the institution or over the phone, then arrange to meet them at a convenient time and place for the actual interview.

The time of day or day of the week may also impact your selection of subjects because it may determine who is available to be approached. Especially if you are sampling subjects from a much larger pool, be aware of the institution's pattern of use. For example, it's not unusual for school groups to visit a museum on weekday mornings and for families to come during the weekend. Families with young children may come mainly on weekend mornings to avoid afternoon nap times. Thus, if you are studying family groups, you may want to sample during the weekend hours. If you are trying to generalize to all types of casual visitors, however, you should select subjects during all hours of active visitation. Most informal institutions have collected data on use patterns, or security personnel may know what these patterns are.

Table 5 shows an example of a plan to select subjects from a pool of casual visitors to a museum that is open seven days a week from 10:00 A.M. to 5:00 P.M. In this case, the hours from 3:00 P.M. to 5:00 P.M. were avoided because subjects would be tired near the end of their visit. At another museum, or in a different study, there might be good reasons for sampling during this time.

Table 5. An example of how a matrix can be used to assist in choosing balanced sampling times.

	M	T	W	Th	F	Sa	Su
Morning							
10 A.M. – 12 NOON		x		x		x	
Afternoon							
1 P.M. – 3 P.M.	x		x		x		x
3 P.M. – 5 P.M.							

Selecting Subjects for Qualitative Studies

Qualitative evaluations often require small numbers of subjects that are selected for specific reasons. Typical qualitative sampling methods include the following (from Patton 1987:52–57):

- *Extreme case sampling*: Choose unusual or special cases to shed light on why things do or do not work for particular individuals. Choose the best-case or worst-case example.

- *Maximum variation sampling*: Capture central themes and principal outcomes by selecting diverse characteristics for constructing the sample. If the program covers a broad geographical area, then select subjects that represent the region's major features (e.g., rural, urban, suburban); if the program reaches diverse audiences, make sure that diversity is represented in the subjects.

- *Homogeneous sampling*: Pick a small sample that focuses on a particular issue of importance, for example adults over sixty or children between three and five years of age.

- *Typical case sampling*: Using the help of people who know what "typical" really is, choose subjects that are as close to that ideal as possible. If most of the visitors are family groups with two parents and two children, then the sample might include only these groups.

- *Critical case sampling*: Critical cases are those that are very important for some reason. For example, if your graphics can be read by a group of visitors over sixty years of age, then most other age groups can probably read them as well.

- *Chain sampling*: In this approach, one subject refers you to another subject, who then refers you to another, each providing their own perspective on the issue of concern.

- *Informants*: One or more people serve to provide you with ongoing information about a situation or program. For example, a docent or volunteer may be willing to serve as an informant to relay detailed information about the volunteer program from the perspective of a participant.

Sometimes you may seek what Patton (1987) calls "confirming cases," in which you look for subjects who might present a similar view to those you have already collected. For example, if disabled visitors in your sample encountered problems using the exhibits, then you may want to seek out other disabled subjects to confirm their experiences. There are instances in which you may sample cases for political reasons, for example including a board member or administrator as an interview subject. Participation in the interview can have the secondary, and desirable, effect of informing and reassuring that person about the nature of the study. Finally, there are always occasions in which time or resources are simply limited, so you end up sampling whomever is available and take into account possible sources of bias as you examine the findings.

Chapter 4

Observational Tools

Counting Heads

The most basic kind of observational data is a number count of people. You can obtain a profile of your visitors by counting who comes in the door on various days and times. You can determine the composition of visitor groups in order to determine whether people visit primarily as family groups or with their peers. You may want to know whether the numbers of visitors differ by time of day or day of the week. A count of the numbers of people who visit different exhibits can indicate differences in their popularity, ease of use, or accessibility within the museum. Counting visitors can also serve as a first step toward more in-depth studies.

Counting visitors begins with the following steps:

- Determine how you will inform the visitors that the research project is occurring. Generally, a sign at the entrance of the museum informing people about the nature and reason for the research is sufficient when you are only counting numbers of people that enter the institution. If possible, let visitors know that they can request to be excluded from the count.

- Decide how you will collect your data. You may choose to count visitors as they enter the building, but you should also investigate whether there are easier ways to gather the data. Passive methods for counting visitors, such as an automatic turnstile or a tabulating electric eye, may already exist in the institution. Sometimes the museum's entrance-fee structure will allow you to infer visitation from each day's gate return or from the quantity of distributed tickets.

- Decide when and where you will make your counts. Try to sample regularly enough so you do not bias your count with just afternoon visitors or just weekend visitors. Sometimes it is possible for the staff at each entrance to count and categorize every person who enters the museum.

- Construct a data collection form using the following categories: date, time, name of the person doing the counting, subject's sex, and group type (adult-child, adult only, child only), age estimate (child 1–20, adult 21–40, middle adult 41–60, older adult 61–80, 81–100). For more detail on children, subdivide that category (preschool 1–5, elementary 6–10, preteen 11–15, young adult 16–20). University museums should add "college student only" to the group-type category.

Tracking Movements

Tracking visitors' movements within a museum or exhibition can give you an idea of what exhibits or objects are attended. Sometimes the spatial arrangement of an area can encourage or discourage access to particular features. During the 1920s and 1930s, Arthur Melton (1933, 1935) and Edward Robinson (1928, 1931) and their colleagues

tracked the movements of visitors in museums and identified several consistent patterns of spatial use. These researchers observed that, all other things being equal, visitors tended
to turn right when entering galleries, they tended to follow the right-hand wall, and they tended to spend less time
at exhibits as they approached the exit. Very popular
exhibits had paradoxical effects on the surrounding exhibits—sometimes they had spillover effects, encouraging
visitors to use the exhibits nearby, while in other instances
they overshadowed surrounding exhibits, making them vir-
tually invisible to the public. These findings have been confirmed by various researchers since that time (for a review
of this issue, see Serrell 1997). Figure 3 shows one method
of how tracking data can be displayed.

To track the movements of visitors, begin by using a
simplified floor plan of the museum gallery to record the
pattern of each subject's movements. Here are some guidelines:

- Record only one subject's movements on a single floor
  plan. An active subject will provide a sufficiently
  complex pattern for interpretation. If you wish to follow
  family groups, then choose one member to be your focal
  subject and record that person's behavior in detail and
  indicate with general notes the movement of the rest
  of the group.

- You may record the time spent at various locations.
  Indicate those locations in advance by circling the area
  on your floor plan. You can fill in the circle with a time
  value (the length of time spent at the location) as you
  make your recording. Don't include more locations
  than is practical to record with an active subject.

- You may record a code for the behavior of visitors at
  particular stations (figure 4). Indicate those locations

Figure 3. The flow pattern of visitors through the Origin of Species exhibit at the British Museum (Natural History). The patterns are expressed as percentages (n=140 visitors). The floor area was approximately 840 square meters (Griggs 1983:124).

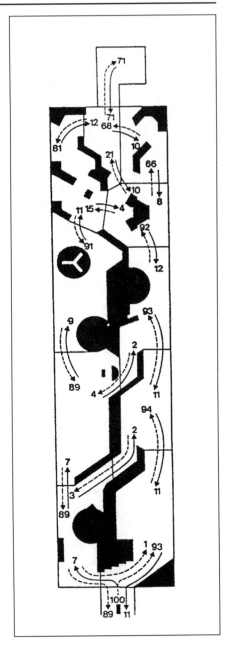

le	look at exhibit only
man	manipulate exhibit
tk	talk to person
ce	comment, exhibit related
cg	comment related to graphic/text
qe	question, exhibit related
tn	talk, not exhibit related
lat	look at label/graphic
ra	read label aloud
nn	none of the above

Figure 4. Some behaviors and possible codes to use when making brief observations.

by drawing a square on your floor plan in advance. Again, don't include more locations than is practical to follow with an active subject, or you will not be able to collect accurate data. Depending on the type of exhibit, you may be limited in how detailed the codes should be. Include those codes that give the information that is most important to you. Be sure to make the codes descriptive of observable behaviors. For example, you may not be able to verify whether a subject has read the exhibit label, unless they read it aloud. Therefore, you might want to use the categories "looked at label" and "read label aloud." If there was no time to make a notation about behavior at a given station, then leave the box blank.

Make enough tracking maps to have a good represen-tation of the possible patterns of use of the exhibit or mu-seum. Then sort them into possible patterns. Use your own judgment as to what categories would be useful to sort the tracking maps. Some examples are:

- *Heavy, medium, and light use*: Select typical examples that show variations in how many of the available exhibits the subjects visit and interact with. Heavy use involves a lot of interaction at many different exhibits. Light use may reflect very little time spent at the exhibits, few exhibits visited, or both.

- *Complete and incomplete visits*: Sometimes a visitor stops at every station or exhibit, skipping very few of the available opportunities for interaction. This can be considered a "complete," or thorough pattern. Contrast the most complete patterns you find with those that short-circuit the visit in various ways. Look for tracing patterns that show areas of the gallery or museum that are ignored when visitors decide to move on.

- *Fast and slow visits*: Some visitors are thorough but spend very little time at any one exhibit. Contrast this pattern with those in which visitors spend lots of time at some or all of the exhibits. Don't hesitate to create intermediate categories to show the more typical patterns.

- *Intensive, focused, and minimal use*: Intensive use might refer to a long time spent at relatively few exhibits. Focused use might refer to a moderate amount of time spent at very few exhibits. Minimal use might refer to a short time at very few exhibits.

Brief Observations

Sometimes it is helpful to make relatively brief observations of what visitors are doing in an institution or program. Such observations do not give a lot of detail about the behavior of subjects, and they don't always generalize to the larger audience. They can, however, gather useful information for the design of new exhibits or programs.

Brief observations are an essential tool for conducting formative evaluations of exhibits and programs. The term *formative evaluation* refers to studies that occur while programs or exhibits are being designed. Typically, visitors are asked to interact with a version of the exhibit that has not yet been completed. The formative evaluation provides information that will assist the designer in predicting how well the idea of the exhibit or program will work for visitors. The better the quality of the data collected, the more likely the results will be a good predictor of the future appeal of the exhibit or program. A useful reference for formative evaluations is *Try It! Improving Exhibits through Formative Evaluation*, edited by Samuel Taylor.

Brief observations can be made using descriptions, text, design drawings, or models. They are most effective, however, when the item being studied is as close as possible to the final product. It is not usually cost-effective to make a finished exhibit for brief observations, because the purpose is to identify changes that should be made in the exhibit, and finishing exhibits is a cost- and time-intensive process. It is often practical, however, to make a rough working version of the exhibit. This is called a prototype. According to David Taylor, a prototype is

> either a mock-up of the exhibit—a version made out
> of inexpensive and disposable materials—or a first
> version of the exhibit, one not yet finished. Likewise,
> early versions of labels can be considered to be
> prototypes and can be evaluated in the same fashion
> as mechanical devices. As soon as any part of the
> exhibit is in a form that visitors can use, evaluation
> can begin. (1991:33)

While study subjects interact with an exhibit prototype, the evaluator makes brief observations of how well the exhibit seems to work. Usually a short interview follows the observations, although the evaluator may interrupt the observations at points to ask brief questions. Brief observations can be as casual as placing a partially completed exhibit in a public space and watching how people interact with it. The Exploratorium pioneered the method of setting rough versions of exhibits into the public areas of the museum just outside the shop.

> The first stage of exhibit design is the construction of a full-scale working prototype. Reactions to the prototype help the exhibit builder modify and improve the exhibit. The final version of the exhibit is often built around the material in the prototype. As a result, functional considerations and the phenomenon to be displayed dictate the nature and size of the exhibit. (Oppenheimer 1986:28)

At the Exploratorium, the exhibit development area (the shop) is separated from the public areas by only a low, screened wall. The exhibit developers can watch across the shop gate to see how visitors interact with the exhibits, and they occasionally go out and ask people questions. The tone of the whole process is casual and flexible, with an emphasis on gaining insight into how to make improvements in the exhibits that will help people's interactions and understanding.

Brief observations can also be more structured. In one study, we arranged for a small group of elementary school students to interact with a prototype of a multimedia exhibit about searching for fossils (Diamond et al. 1995). The students used the exhibit at regular intervals throughout the course of development. At each session, individual students were observed and interviewed as they watched digitized video and played computer games. Later, we assembled groups of experts and novices to see how they differed from each other in their reactions to the prototypes.

Some researchers have questioned whether people's responses to an unfinished exhibit will approximate those to the finished version. Steven Griggs and Jane Manning (1983) investigated whether visitors at the British Museum (Natural History) in London reacted differently to models than to complete versions of the Hall of Human Biology's Living Cells exhibit. They concluded that the models were generally good predictors of visitor behavior at the finished version of the exhibits.

To make brief observations, first consider who your subjects will be. To get the best indication of how the exhibit will be used, include the most diverse subjects possible in your sample pool: the tallest, the shortest, non-English speaking, disabled, subject-matter experts, and complete novices. The greater the diversity of your sample, the more likely your brief observations will hold true for a larger audience.

Be opportunistic, seeking out your subjects wherever they are available. During an evaluation of a multimedia exhibit, we wanted to make sure that the placement of the computer trackball, button, and screen was comfortable for visitors, particularly for parents with young children. After observing a variety of subjects with the prototype, we invited a staff member to try it out with his young twins. Both twins sat on his lap and attempted to work the exhibit at the same time. One of the twins was a dwarf, and his father attempted to make sure that he could reach the controls as easily as his brother could. This particular case provided us with a wealth of ideas on how to modify the exhibit design to best meet visitors' specialized needs.

Once you have decided who your subjects are, create a data collection sheet (an example is shown in figure 5). Decide what information about the subjects is important for you to record. Generally it is useful to know your subjects' sex, the type of group they are in, a general idea of their age, what language they use in the museum, and the

```
                    Fossil Identification Evaluation
                         Stage 2: Interview #

Date:

Subject: ()AM ()AF ()FC ()MC ()Family/Group ()Other:

Prototype Description:


Start Time:

Observations:




End Time/obs:
```

```
                              Questions

1.  What was the point (purpose) of this exhibit?


2.  What do you think you are looking at?


3.  Was this activity fun or boring?

4.  Do you have any questions or suggestions?
```

```
Subject: Sex: M  F
Age: ()under 6 ()6-10 ()11-14 ()15-17 ()18-24 ()25-32 ()33-45 ()46+
Group/Family Size: 2 3 4 5 6+
Ethnicity:
Language:
```

Figure 5. A data collection sheet for the formative evaluation of an exhibit on finding and identifying fossils at the University of Nebraska State Museum (Twersky 1994).

nature of any apparent disabilities. This information can usually be obtained from observing the visitors. Note the following steps to brief observations that are used in formative evaluations:

- Give the subjects a quick overview of the purpose of the research, and request their permission to include them as participants.

- Ask the subjects to try out the exhibit, using the labels for assistance. If a subject has children, arrange something for them to do.

- Note what each subject does. Write the descriptions as a narrative or use codes to represent certain actions. If the subject asks you questions while trying out the prototype, do your best to answer them.

- Let the subjects choose when to leave the exhibit.

- As they prepare to leave, ask them a few questions to determine what they thought of the exhibit, what worked or did not work for them, and what their general recommendations are for improving the exhibit. Keep a record of their responses.

- You may want to ask more detailed questions about the exhibit labels. You can prepare different versions of the labels and ask subjects for their preferences. You can also ask subjects to describe in their own words what a label says. Keep a record of their responses.

- Don't prejudge the results. Remain open to what your subjects show or tell you, rather than try to seek evidence to support one view. Researchers and/or staff may have strong ideas about what works and what does not. Nevertheless, it is essential to remain attentive to the perspective that your subjects present, whether or not you agree with it.

• Write up your findings in a concise format (see figure 6).

Recording Detailed Observations

Detailed observations provide information about what visitors actually do in informal educational settings. This method has been used by numerous researchers to understand how informal learning occurs, to understand sex and age differences in out-of-school learning, and perhaps most importantly, to observe how social interactions among museum visitors contribute to the informal learning experience.

Detailed observations have been conducted in museums and other informal educational settings since the studies of Edward Robinson and Arthur Melton in the 1920s and 1930s. Over the years, researchers have conducted detailed observations while following visitors on foot with clipboards (e.g., Diamond 1980), and they have observed them using the footage from security video cameras (Falk 1983). In one study at the National Museum of Natural History, the researchers even hid inside a giant grasshopper exhibit in order to record the details of visitor behavior and conversation (Wiegman and Wiegman 1973). Although current ethics concerns have sharply limited the variety of ways that researchers conduct detailed observations, this nonetheless remains one of the most important ways to gather data about visitors.

The results of detailed observations have had a major impact on how educators view the experience of visiting a museum, zoo, aquarium, or park. Initially, these visits were conceived of as primarily interactions between visitors and exhibits, but two decades of observational studies in these

Wentzscope
Stage 1 Position Evaluation Summary
# of Visitors observed: 69 total

METHODS: Observations were conducted on Friday 5-13-94 between 9:30 a.m. and 2 p.m. Observations were conducted in the Encounter center. The evaluator sat in on 4 classes: 21 first graders; 18 second graders; 13 fourth graders and 17 fifth graders. A total of 65 students and 4 adults (teachers) were observed. The criteria for the observations as to observe every single visitor/child who approached the Wentzscope during the period of time (about 30 minutes) that class was in the Encounter center.

PROTOTYPE DESCRIPTION: The Wentzscope was tested for height positioning, it was therefore secured to a wood platform on an adjustable stool. A 6 foot ruler was placed next to the Wentzscope. The ruler was used to note the visitor's height. The ruler has a .25-.5 inch error margin. The Wentzscope was tested at 3 different levels. Each level was measured for base height and lens height. Base height was measured from the floor to the top of the stool. The lens height was measured from the floor to the lens and includes the 6.75" of space for the light housing. The first base height was at 2 feet (lens height=3'6.5"), the second base height tested was at 2 feet and 2.25 inches (lens height=3'6.5"), the third height tested was at 2 feet and 6.5 inches (lens height=4'1"). The last height allows for a wheelchair that is 2'5.5"+ high to roll directly up to the Wentzscope. A box (7.5 inches high) for stepping on was also provided.

RESULTS: All 69 visitors stood as close to the Wentzscope as possible with their eyes and noses directly on the lens. Therefore, no two visitors were able to use the Wentzscope at the same time. The visitors were very possessive about their time at the Wentzscope and would have spent on average more than 2 minutes if they hadn't been pushed, shoved or yelled out of the way by their classmates. All the visitors knew to move the slide carrier and use the focus knob.

Visitors who were 3'9" to 4'2" in height had to rise to their toes to see through the lens when the lens was at 3'6.5". Visitors who were 4'2" to 4'8" appeared to be comfortable with the lens at 3'6.5" and 3' 8.5" but had to stand on the box or rise to their toes to see the lens at 4'1". Visitors who were 4'10" to 5'0" appeared to be comfortable with the lens at 4'1". Visitors who were 5'1" to 5'2" had to bend slightly to see into the lens at 4'1".

RECOMMENDATIONS: If the base height of the Wentzscope is at 2'6" it will allow a wheelchair to come very close but the lens would be too high for the person in the wheelchair. However, as it was previously suggested by members of the core exhibits team, if the Wentzscope could be tilted by the visitor to a comfortable viewing position then it could still be set at a base height of 2'6". However, if possible, this adjustable viewing mechanism should be tested with people who actually use wheelchairs.

Figure 6. A brief report on the formative evaluation of a Wentzscope exhibit installed in a new gallery on the Age of Dinosaurs at the University of Nebraska State Museum (Twersky 1994).

settings have created a new paradigm for how to view visits to these institutions. The author's own work and that of John Falk, Sherman Rosenfeld, Samuel Taylor, Lynn Dierking, Ross Loomis, and many others have created an awareness of the central importance of visitors' social interactions in informal learning. These studies have shown that social experience is often a primary motivation for the visits, and that social interaction is a fundamental part of the teaching and learning. A useful reference that summarizes what is known about the role of social behavior in informal educational settings is *The Museum Experience*, by John H. Falk and Lynn D. Dierking (1992).

Conducting detailed observations requires decisions about which recording equipment, which observational categories, and what behavioral sampling technique to use. More information about recording detailed behavior can be found in *Measuring Behavior*, by Paul Martin and Patrick Bateson (1988), and in *Quantitative Methods in the Study of Animal Behavior*, by Brian A. Hazlett.

Recording Equipment

A data-collection sheet and a stopwatch are usually sufficient equipment for recording brief observations. Once you decide to make detailed recordings of behavior, however, some extra technology can be helpful. Data can be collected using an event recorder, a tape recorder, or a video camera. Event recorders can be simple mechanical devices with a built-in timer and a numerical keyboard, or they can be laptop computers that will record the intervals between keyboard notations to the millisecond. When collecting detailed behavioral data in the field, I generally use a laptop computer with a custom-designed recording program, while the computer's clock keeps track of time intervals. There are now several commercially available programs that will convert your laptop into a behavioral event recorder.

A tape recorder can also be used as a data-collection device. One can record visitors' comments in an interview or their conversations during observations. Generally, however, written permission from subjects must be obtained before direct recordings are made. Alternatively, the investigator can speak quietly into the tape recorder, giving an ongoing description of the behaviors observed. Since the tape records at real time, no separate timing mechanism is required.

Videotape can produce an even more detailed record, although, like audiotape, it requires written permission from subjects. Video cameras capture both behaviors and conversations, and also make identification of subjects relatively easy. In order to decide which equipment to use for recording your data, you should consider the following:

- *Amount of data*: Check sheets collect the least amount of data, while video cameras generally capture the most.

- *Subjects' comfort*: Subjects often pay little attention to an observer holding a pad of paper or clipboard. They are more wary of someone using a small electronic event recorder or talking into a tape recorder. They can be quite self-conscious and uncomfortable being videotaped.

- *Ease of transcription*: Observational notes such as narrative or written codes generally take about the same amount of time to transcribe as the behavior they record lasted. Thus it takes about an hour to transcribe an hour's worth of written observational notes. Transcription time increases greatly with more advanced recording devices. For example, it takes about four hours to transcribe an hour's worth of notes on a tape recorder. It takes about sixteen hours to transcribe an hour's worth of videotape. Ease of transcription from event recorders will vary with the equipment involved. Computer programs can be written to translate the data directly into a form that can be analyzed. Sometimes you do not need to transcribe data records completely. Audio or video recordings are sometimes kept just for review or presentation, and the data for analysis are collected in more compact forms.

- *Affordability*: Check sheets cost the price of paper and copy charges. Tape recorders for talking into (but not for producing quality recordings of others' conversations) can be purchased for under $100. Video cameras, battery packs, and tripods are available for under $1,000. A laptop computer and event-recording software may run to several thousand dollars.

Figure 7 compares the various data collection devices. Not surprisingly, any choice of recording device represents some kind of compromise.

Observation Categories

The first step in making detailed observations is to create a sample ethogram. The word *ethogram* was popularized by the Nobel Prize–winning biologist Konrad Lorenz; it refers to the sum total of an animal's behavioral repertoire (Lorenz 1950). The concept is used widely by biologists who record the behavior of wild animals in their natural habitat. An ethogram is a list of the major categories of behavior of which a species is capable. Conducting observations of visitors in a museum or zoo has many similarities to observing wild animals in nature. In both settings,

	Amount of data	Subjects' comfort	Ease of transcription	Affordability
Check sheets	medium	high	high (1:1)	high
Event recorder	high	medium to low	medium to high	low to medium
Audio tape	high	medium	medium (1:4)	medium
Videotape	highest	low	low (1:16)	low

Figure 7. Comparisons between various recording devices used in evaluation studies (modified from Diamond 1982:15). High values are more desirable. Numbers in parentheses indicate the ratio of recording time to transcription time.

the observer tries to record the natural behavior of the subject, with minimal influence by the researcher. A museum or zoo ethogram is a list of the behavioral categories that visitors display while they are in those settings. Follow these steps to construct an ethogram:

- Conduct a series of preliminary observations during which you make a list of all of the behaviors you see your subjects display. You can add other behaviors you may have observed earlier, even if they do not occur in the preliminary sessions. You may choose to begin with lists of behaviors that have been published by other researchers, then modify them by observing the particular audience you plan to study.

- Define each behavior explicitly, so that it can only mean specified actions. Behaviors should be described on the basis of observable features; do not include behaviors that require you to guess what the subject is feeling.

Earlier, I mentioned that you cannot tell if a subject is reading the exhibit labels unless she reads aloud. In my studies, I use two categories, "look at label" and "read label aloud." Sometimes these are summarized in a single category called "read label," although this still only means that the subject either looked at the label or read it to someone else. Similarly, you can observe a subject smiling, but you can't observe whether she is happy. Therefore, "smile" is the more appropriate category.

- Be aware of whether your behavioral categories are events or states. Some kinds of analysis will require you to use only one or the other. *Events* are behavior patterns of relatively short duration, such as "touch," "ask question," "hit," or "read aloud." *States* are behavior patterns of generally long duration, such as "rest," "wait," and "sit."

- Decide whether you will measure latency, frequency, duration, or intensity:

    Latency is the time it takes before the first occurrence of a behavior. Latency can be timed from a variable in the environment or it can be signaled by the subject's own actions, for example the time from when a visitor first approaches an exhibit to when she starts to use it.

    Frequency is the number of occurrences of a behavior per unit of time. For example, it can refer to how often children engage in nontask behavior during a program.

    Duration is the length of time of a single occurrence of the behavior pattern. For example, it can be how long visitors manipulate an exhibit.

Intensity is a graded measure of behavior. For example, movement could be rated "run," "fast walk," or "slow walk;" the frequency of each speed category would then be recorded.

- Specify the time period that your observations will last. For example, it could be from when the visitor first approaches the exhibit to when she leaves.

- Code your behavioral categories in a way that is easy for you to remember. It is usually easier to remember categories that are abbreviated in two- or three-letter codes (lat = look at, man = manipulate exhibit) than categories that are given numerical designations.

Typically, ethograms involve long lists of behavior categories. Figure 8 shows an ethogram of seventy categories that was used by the author (Diamond 1980, 1986) in her study of family groups at the Exploratorium and the Lawrence Hall of Science. Each category is defined in terms of observable behaviors.

Sometimes, however, it is more practical to use shorter lists of behaviors. Figures 9 and 10 provide examples of shorter behavioral coding schemes that have been used to record social behaviors in museums.

The list of behavioral codes is the vocabulary of behavioral observations. Just as you might construct sentences from word lists, observers construct behavioral descriptions from the list of behavioral categories. The exact record of what the subject is observed to do is recorded as "sentences" made up of the category codes or in columns of single categories. Most often, when the notes are taken by hand, the behavioral categories are abbreviated with one or two letter codes, so that they can be recorded quickly.

CONDENSED BEHAVIOR CATEGORIES

1. APPROACH FIRST

2. APPROACH SECOND

3. ASK FOR HELP
   a. Ask for help
   b. Express inability to do exhibit

4. COMFORT
   a. Be helped with shoes
   b. Comfort carry or hold hands
   c. Comfort touch
   d. Comfort verbal
   e. Help person with shoes
   f. Tell not museum related

5. DISTRESS/AGGRESS
   a. Complain about person
   b. Cry or scream
   c. Hit
   d. Yell

6. FAVORABLE COMMENT
   a. Express ability to do exhibit
   b. Express like
   c. Refer to future exhibit interaction
   d. Reminisce about exhibit

7. INTERACT OUTSIDE GROUP
   a. Look at explainer manipulate
   b. Manipulate exhibit w/non-group
      person
   c. Verbal from explainer
   d. Verbal from non-group person
   e. Verbal to explainer
   f. Verbal to non-group person
   g. Verbal to observer

8. LOOK AT GRAPHICS

9. MANIPULATE ALONE
   a. Hold exhibit
   b. Manipulate attempt
   c. Manipulate exhibit
   d. Manipulate go inside
   e. Manipulate incorrectly
   f. Manipulate look
   g. Verbal to exhibit

10. MANIPULATE TOGETHER
    a. Ask to join
    b. Manipulate exhibit together
    c. Manipulate together incorrectly
    d. Relate new exhibit rule

11. NAME EXHIBIT
    a. Describe exhibit briefly
    b. Name exhibit
    c. Name other museum structure
    d. Refer to school or home with exhibit

12. OBSERVE PERSON
    a. Look at person manipulate
    b. Photograph person manipulating

13. QUESTION ABOUT CONTENT

14. QUESTION ABOUT INTERACTION

15. READ ALOUD

16. RELATE/DESCRIBE
    a. Describe exhibit in detail
    b. Relate exhibit

17. SHOW
    a. Hand exhibit to person
    b. Hold exhibit up for person to see
    c. Lift person to exhibit
    d. Manipulate repeat for person
    e. Move person to exhibit
    f. Point to exhibit
    g. Pull person to exhibit
    h. Tell to come

18. TELL
    a. Tell to do
    b. Tell to do not
    c. Tell to manipulate
    d. Tell to observe
    e. Tell to read
    f. Tell to think or guess

19. TERMINATE
    a. Ask to leave
    b. Move exhibit from person
    c. Move person from exhibit
    d. Tell to go

20. UNFAVORABLE COMMENT
    a. Express dislike
    b. Express want to go home

21. WITHDRAW
    a. Leave exhibit
    b. Look away

Figure 8. *This ethogram includes seventy behavior categories that describe visitor interactions at the Exploratorium and the Lawrence Hall of Science. The seventy categories are then grouped statistically into twenty-one more general categories (Diamond 1980:41).*

VISUAL INFORMATION SEEKING
1. Look/read: Looks at objects, looks intently, focuses on panel, reads to self.
2. Watch others: Watching others' behavior at the exhibit, or watching over another's shoulder.

VERBAL INFORMATION SEEKING AND EXCHANGE
3. Verbal plus: Asks questions, gives explanations, interprets, attempts to verify, relates to other concepts or instances, says "very interested," makes sound effects, smiles, laughs, appears awestruck, says is good, says is bad, "Ahah!," etc.
4. Verbal: Identifies, says what sees, points out or says where is, simply describes, reads aloud, states facts, etc.

ACTIVE MANIPULATION/MANUAL EXPLORATION
5. Do/manipulate: Manipulates exhibit appropriately, engages in looking or speaking behaviors as required.
6. Touch: Touch with evident intent to experience/feel.

OTHER BEHAVIORS
7. Gaze/move: Gazes at exhibit, moves on while looking.
8. Orient/fatigue: Orients to exhibition environment or family members, gazes about, leans, sits in exhibition area, wiggles/fidgets, exits, etc.
9. Not exhibit related: Fills out questionnaires, makes plans, chats, etc.
10. Misc.: Ambiguous behaviors and unknown behaviors at the observation station.

Transcript Segment

Site	Time	# at Exh.	# at Site	Comment:
12	2:53	26	9	Boy operates/reads while Mom watches reads over his shoulder; also three girls watch and two other adults, and a teenage boy and an extra boy watch; boy leaves, and girls dive in to operate it. Girl (8-10) watches/does computer carefully; small boy (6) seems awestruck by sounds/colors but soon fidgets as watches. Teenage boy watches/reads. The girl doing computer is quite relaxed, interested. Adult male joins wife at computer. She says " . . .look at that, that laser goes right through that . . .," girl leaves.

Coding of Transcript Segment

Boy operates/reads while Mom watches/reads over his shoulder	...(CHILD MALE do, read) ...(ADULT FEMALE read)
Also three girls watch	...(3 CHILD FEMALE X watch)
and two other adults, and	
a teenage boy and an	...(2 ADULT?SEX X watch)
extra boy watch	...(TEEN CHILD watch)
	...(CHILD MALE watch)
Boy leaves and girls dive in to	...(CHILD MALE [exit] orient/fatigue)
operate it	...(3 CHILD FEMALE X do)
Girl (8-10) reads/does computer carefully	...(CHILD read+, do+)

Figure 9. The upper portion shows the categories used to code transcripts of observed visitor behavior at the traveling computer exhibit Laser at 25, at the Maryland Science Center and the Discovery Center in Fort Lauderdale. The lower portion gives a sample from the initial transcript for a single observation (Hilke et al. 1988:40).

```
FORMAT:_____
                attention to     subject     verb      child



ATTENTION TO:
(1)     exhibit
(2)     setting
(3)     self
(4)     own social group
(5)     other social group

SUBJECT:
(1)     Mother
(2)     Father

VERB:
(1)     disciplines
(2)     points out specimen
(3)     points out aspect of specimen
(4)     questions
(5)     answers
(6)     explains
(7)     manages
(8)     reinforces
(9)     does not interact
(10)    cannot tell
(11)    listens to child
(12)    engages in a related conversation
(13)    engages in an unrelated conversation

CHILD:
(11)    oldest male
(12)    second oldest male
(13)    third oldest male
(14)    fourth oldest male
(21)    oldest female
(22)    second oldest female
(23)    third oldest female
(24)    fourth oldest female
(1)     more than one child
(2)     other adult
(3)     child-child interactions
```

Figure 10. This instrument allows the evaluator to use coded "sentences" to describe interactions between parents and children at museum exhibits (Dierking 1987:37).

Behavior Sampling Methods

Your next step for organizing your detailed observations is to choose your behavioral sampling method. Since the behavior of a subject unfolds in a continuous stream of information and activity, the observer needs to decide how to select, or sample, from the continuous flow. The most commonly used method of sampling behavior is called "focal individual sampling." In this method, the observer chooses a single individual and observes her behavior for the duration of the session. When the focal subject is out of sight, the observations are stopped until she returns.

Observations of social behaviors can be made with focal individual sampling by noting all the interactions a subject has with other people. When observing family groups, you can choose to observe one person per group whose characteristics are decided in advance (e.g., adult female). Since family groups do not always stay together, this will allow a consistent record of one individual's behavior. If you are fairly sure, however, that two people will stay together, you can use focal dyad sampling, in which you record the behavior of a pair of subjects, such as a parent and child.

When using focal individual sampling, the observer typically records a continuous stream of behaviors in an attempt to make the most complete record possible. This is called "continuous recording." A beginning and end time is usually specified in advance. For example, the first approach of a child to an exhibit could signal the beginning of a continuous recording session, and her exit from the exhibit could signal the end. This type of recording is most feasible when you make a video record of an event, and then replay that record for detailed, sometimes even frame-by-frame, analysis. An audio record of behavior can work the same way; you can speak a continuous description of behavioral events into a tape recorder for later transcription. Continuous recording is also possible on a laptop computer, using a program that automatically keeps track of time. In formative evaluation, it is possible to do a rough version of continuous recording by exposing a subject to an exhibit, and then using codes to record a continuous description of what the subject does. Although the recording may not be in great detail, it may accurately represent how the subject used the exhibit; this information can be a valuable source of information for the exhibit designers.

With focal individual sampling, it is also possible to select a unit of time and then record what behaviors are occurring at the end of each interval. This is called "time sampling." For example, you might note at five-minute intervals whether the subject is active or resting. Recording this data throughout the course of the visit might help you determine where resting stations should be located. For time sampling, the behaviors usually are noted ahead of time on a check sheet, and at each interval time is entered next to the appropriate behavior. In a variation on this technique, called "one-zero sampling," the observer notes the presence or absence of a behavior at regular intervals. One-zero sampling is most useful when the sampling interval is relatively frequent, such as each minute.

Focal individual sampling may not be the best choice when a lot of data on individual subjects is not needed. An alternative technique, "scan sampling," records the behavior of all members of an entire group at regular intervals. For example, every thirty minutes you could note what each individual in a single museum gallery is doing. Over the course of the day, this sample would provide a rough measure of visitor behavior in that gallery. Because scan sampling has to occur quickly, however, it is often biased toward highly visible behaviors and thus may not provide an accurate representation of what visitors actually do.

Another method of selecting what to observe is called "behavior sampling." In this technique, the observer watches a group of subjects and then records each occurrence of a particular behavior. The observer usually also notes something about the context for that behavior, who was involved, or at which exhibit it occurred. For example, an observer may stand at one exhibit and record the length of time each visitor spends looking at the labels. This may give a rough idea of how much attention is given to the label, and by whom. Behavior sampling is usually used to study behaviors that are relatively infrequent.

When making preliminary observations to generate the behavioral categories, an observer may use "ad libitum sampling." In this sampling method, the observer records whatever is visible and interesting at any time; there is no set schedule for making the observations. The method may also be used during participant observation, when the observer may be a part of the activity being observed. In this case, the observer takes notes as she is able. Sometimes ad lib sampling is useful during an uncommon or unpredictable event, such as the appearance of a famous or entertaining person, an unusually large crowd, or an emergency such as an earthquake.

Validity and Reliability

It is important to know that the means of assessment you have developed is accurate and appropriate. This is what is usually referred to as validity in research. If you are using a series of behaviors to determine whether learning has occurred, then you need to be sure that the behaviors are valid indicators of learning. If a subject is observed looking at a label, that is not the same as reading, so to call it reading behavior would have poor validity. Validity is always an issue in research, whether you are conducting observations, interviews, questionnaires, or tests. Basically, if the data are consistent with outside experts' notions of what an instrument should be measuring, then it is more likely to be valid. According to Roger Miles,

> In evaluation research, which is usually concerned with practical issues independent of theory, the best one can do is to find an outside criterion against which the measuring instrument can be verified. For example, if an instrument has been designed to measure the extent to which different exhibits are able to increase learning on a given topic among visitors, an idea of its validity would be gained by the extent to which "expert" teachers independently agreed with the instrument's assessment of "successful" and "unsuccessful" exhibits. (Miles et al. 1988:164)

There are several ways to ensure that your instruments are valid:

- Conduct informal observations to determine the nature and complexity of the environment you are studying.

- Generate categories of behavior from the environment you are working in. One common mistake in informal education is to use categories of behavior that have been generated from school environments. When those categories are applied to a playground, zoo, or museum, they may lack validity because they are not measuring what is intended. Similarly, in interviews and questionnaires, using questions that are generated from the environment you are studying can protect validity.

- Make periodic reviews of the environment you are studying. Make sure you know what is on the exhibit labels and what exhibits are on the floor on the day that you are recording your data. If you are at a zoo, make sure you know what animals are currently on display; at botanic gardens, know what plants are visible. At a playground, make sure you know what equipment is available.

Reliability is a measure of how consistent a research method is. A reliable method measures the same thing, usually in the same way, each time it is used. Reliability is influenced by the method's precision (is it free from random errors?), by its sensitivity (does it respond to small changes?) and by its resolution (how small a difference will it notice?). A behavioral category that is poorly defined may not be reliable because it may indicate different behavior patterns each time it is used. An interview question that is asked a different way each time may not be reliable because it elicits a different kind of response.

The degree to which an instrument is reliable can be measured and evaluated statistically through a variety of different methods. Generally, in observational studies there are two kinds of reliability, inter- and intra-observer reliability. To measure inter-observer reliability, at least two different observers should watch the same subject using the same behavioral categories and recording technique. You can then measure the association or correlation among the observers' records, typically using either a Pearson correlation coefficient or a Spearman rank correlation coefficient. A correlation of +1.0 usually means a perfect positive correlation between the two responses, while a correlation of zero means that there is no association between the records. A value of 0.6 or greater is normally an acceptable reliability coefficient in naturalistic observational studies.

A second kind of reliability is intra-observer reliability. It is a measure of how consistently the same observer uses an instrument, and whether a single observer will obtain similar results when measuring the same behavior on different occasions. Paul Martin and Patrick Bateson (1988) recommend that the observer videotape a behavioral sequence, then record the behavior while viewing the tape at least two times. As in inter-observer reliability, the correlation between the two records can be measured and evaluated statistically.

You can ensure the reliability of your data by using the following guidelines:

- Make sure that the observer is in a similar condition each time that observations are made. Don't observe when you are sick or tired on one day and in good condition on another.

- Don't let too much time pass between observations. If you are observing visitors at a museum, conduct your observations at frequent intervals. It is best not to let weeks or months go by between observations because both the kinds of visitors and the exhibits can change dramatically.

- Make sure your behavioral categories are clear and unambiguous. If you use codes to record behavioral actions, make sure you use the same codes each time.

- If your raw data is to be transferred into another format (transcribed from tape, typed into a computer), be sure you make the transfer as soon after the original observations as possible.

- Keep your recording method the same each time you observe. If you use a clipboard, then use it every time. Don't talk into a tape recorder on one occasion and take photographs on another. Don't allow friends or associates to watch you on some occasions and not on others.

- Keep your appearance more or less the same throughout your study so that the influence you are having on your subjects remains relatively consistent. Don't dress in formal clothes for one session and in casual ones on another. It is best to look as consistently inconspicuous as possible, which usually means you should dress like a typical museum, zoo, or park visitor.

Participant Observation

Quantitative methods for observing people's behavior assume that the observer is objective. That is, the observer basically tries to remain inconspicuous, exerting minimal influence on the subjects' actions. Participant observation, on the other hand, uses the observer's presence as an advantage in collecting information. As an active participant in an activity, the observer provides an insider's perspective. According to Michael Quinn Patton,

> In participant observation the evaluator shares as intimately as possible in the life and activities of the people in the program. The purpose of such participation is to develop an insider's view of what is happening. This means that the evaluator not only sees what is happening but also feels what it is like to be part of the group.

> Experiencing an environment as an insider is what necessitates the participant part of participant observation. At the same time, however, there is clearly an observer side to this process. The challenge is to combine participation and observation so as to become capable of understanding the experience as an insider while describing the experience for outsiders. (1987:75)

Participant observation originated from the tradition of anthropologists who were studying other cultures and immersing themselves into the experience of those cultures, sometimes for as long as several years. In program evaluation, participant observation can involve relatively short exposure times, with various levels of involvement. In an evaluation of a docent or volunteer program, the evaluator may choose to undergo training and begin to perform volunteer activities, effectively becoming a member of the volunteer group. Similarly, the evaluator may choose to enroll in a class or experience a program with family or friends. The key to participant evaluation is immersion, so that the evaluator can feel what it is like to be a member of the group being studied.

Because of age, sex, background, or ethnicity, the evaluator may not always have the option for full participation in an activity. This can sometimes be rectified when the evaluator includes individuals who belong to the groups being studied as members of the research team. Some situations, however, won't afford that opportunity. Patton (1987:76) describes the following exchange between a prisoner and a young evaluator who was doing participant observation in a prison:

> *Inmate*: "What you here for, man?"
>
> *Evaluator*: "I'm here for a while to find out what's it like to be in prison."
>
> *Inmate*: "What do you mean—'find out what it's like'?"
>
> *Evaluator*: "I'm here so I can experience prison from the inside instead of just studying what it's like from out there."
>
> *Inmate*: "You got to be jerkin' me off, man. Experience from the inside? Shit, man. You can go home when you decide you've had enough can't you?"
>
> *Evaluator*: "Yeah."
>
> *Inmate*: "Then you ain't never gonna know what it's like from the inside."

One way a participant observer can extend her experience is to use informants. As described in chapter 3, informants are members of the group being studied who provide the evaluator with inside information. For example, if you were studying how well a particular institution serves disabled children, you might identify one or more disabled children who would agree to provide you with detailed information about their experiences. Informants should be fairly typical members of the group being studied, and they should be verbal enough to relate their experiences in detail. Sometimes a teacher or staff member can identify potential informants for an evaluator.

Robert Wolf and Barbara Tymitz (1978:6–8) describe five types of data that are often important to the participant observer:

- *Descriptive data about settings.* Record observations about the physical or institutional setting surrounding the situation. Record only what you see and know. Be aware of the difference between fact and impression.

- *Accurate descriptions of actions and behaviors.* Record exactly what is done that relates to the situation you are investigating.

- *Quotable quotes.* Record the key words in a train of thought or discussion exactly as they are stated. Notice the discussion's general flow as well as specifics. You need to pick out exactly what is said and by whom. As much as possible, block out your feelings about what is happening. Reason and emotion only get in the way at this point. You can interpret the data later. Aim for direct quotes as much as possible, since they provide the best material for later analysis. The best way to do this is to listen and take abbreviated notes, then isolate yourself immediately afterward and reconstruct what was said and done.

- *Traces*. These are indicators of past behavior, or accumulations or deposits of evidence providing clues to some past activity. They may include newspaper articles, policy and planning statements, long-range plans, demographic data, guidebooks, governmental regulations, budgets, grant proposals and relevant memos.

- *Wear spots*. Notice any measures of use of particular equipment or activities. Worn rugs might indicate the popularity of various parts of an exhibit.

The signs that visitors leave throughout the museum can be quite subtle. Michael Spock recalls learning about visitors' interests from a janitor:

> He said, "Oh, lots of people look at that exhibit." I said, "I've never seen anybody looking at the exhibit. What's your evidence?" He said, "Well, that's the glass that I have to clean the most in the whole museum. It's just that people don't want you to see them looking at it." (1988:256)

Generally, the participant observer summarizes notes after the activities are over, and these notes become the data record for the evaluation. The notes should contain a thorough description of the program, the feelings and responses of participants as they are conveyed to the evaluator, and the evaluator's own feelings and reactions. How does the program feel? Did you and the other participants want to experience more? What were the components that worked well for you, and which did not? Why do you think certain parts were more successful than others? Whereas objectivity guides other kinds of observations, subjectivity—the key to participant observation—may provide insights that are not accessible with more quantitative techniques.

Chapter 5

Interviews and Questionnaires

Interview Guidelines

Anytime you ask questions of a subject in person, over the phone, even on the Internet, you are conducting an interview. If conducted in a responsible manner, interviews can be excellent tools for assessing visitors' thoughts and experiences.

How questions are asked, however, has a profound influence on the quality of information received. The goal of a well-conducted interview is to elicit a subject's responses in ways that avoid the imposition of bias on the part of the interviewer. A bias-free interview is one in which the subject feels comfortable and safe, where there is no implied prejudgment or criticism by the interviewer, and where the subject feels unhampered in answering the questions in an open and honest manner.

Interviews can involve one subject at a time or groups of subjects. Interviews can be as casual as a conversation or as formal as a list of questions that is prepared in advance and asked in the same manner for each subject. The nature of the interview, however, determines how the findings can be analyzed and constrains the interpretation of the data. Quantitative interviews are relatively formal and structured; the responses are usually analyzed statistically. Qualitative interviews rely more on conversation to probe deeply and to explore interesting new directions; the results are usually presented in narrative form, summarizing major trends or alternatives.

Here are some general guidelines that apply to all kinds of interviews:

- Plan in advance how you will locate and choose your subjects. For lengthy interviews, such as those lasting more than fifteen or twenty minutes, arrange interview times and locations with subjects ahead of time.

- Be honest with the subjects. Tell them the purpose of the interview and seek permission to include them in the study. A tone of openness and honesty is not only ethically appropriate, but it also will make your subject feel comfortable about responding in an open and honest manner.

- Find a place and time for the interview that will be comfortable and convenient for your subjects. Try to arrange for an interview location that provides privacy. If subjects with families are included, make sure you provide supervised activities for young children so they will not distract the subjects. If young children are the focus of the interview, include a means for the caregivers to participate.

- Ask only those questions that are necessary for your study. Any question is an intrusion into the privacy of the subject. Don't ask things unless you are sure you require the answers. Have good reasons for asking questions, especially personal ones.

- When you arrange your questions, order them so the most personal questions come last. Different subjects may have varying ideas of what is considered personal, the interview pay attention to what language the respondent uses to describe the setting, program participants, special activities, or whatever else is reported. The interviewer then uses the language provided by the interviewee in the rest of the interview. Questions that use the respondent's own language are those that are most likely to be clear. (1987:123)

In a long interview, sometimes it is useful to recapitulate what you understand has been said. Recapitulation aids your understanding of the speaker's perspective while you are with the subject, and it can serve as a reliability check. Often it will stimulate the speaker to embellish or clarify the original statement. Robert Wolf and Barbara Tymitz (1978:29) recommend that you begin a recapitulation with one of the following phrases:

So you are saying that . . .
I want to be sure I understand what you are saying . . .
Let me see if I understand what you are telling me . . .

Informal Conversational Interviews

Each kind of interview brings with it advantages and limitations. One of the most common kinds of interviews is the informal conversational interview, or unstructured interview. In this procedure, typical of many qualitative studies, the interviewer allows the nature of the conversation to direct the questioning. After the first several exchanges with the subject, the questions emerge from the course of the discussion. When an important or interesting idea is raised, it may be pursued with follow-up or more in-depth questioning. The subject and interviewer may both play a role in directing the interview, and they may alternate the lead role. Sometimes a subject feels strongly that she wants but typically people are sensitive about giving information about their age, income, and sometimes their name and address. If you require this information for a study, then ask it at the end of the interview. This gives the subjects a chance to get to know you before they are expected to give information that relates most closely to them. Occasionally, a subject will react to a sensitive question by refusing to participate in the interview.

- It is sometimes easier for subjects to place themselves in a category that gives a range of ages or incomes rather than a specific value. For example, instead of asking a subject's age, provide categories that include various age ranges and ask your subjects to indicate the appropriate one. Instead of asking for the subject's annual household income, you could ask, "In which of the following categories does your household income belong? Under $30,000; $30,001 to $60,000; $60,001 to $90,000; over $90,000?"

- Ask about only one item at a time. If you wish to ask about strengths and weaknesses, first ask those questions about one item, then the next. Don't expect the subject to remember several questions phrased as one.

Michael Quinn Patton points out that it is the responsibility of the interviewer to make clear to the subject what is being asked. This requires asking well-phrased questions in a language that the subjects will understand.

In preparing to do an interview, find out what language the people you are interviewing use in talking about the program being studied. Use language that is understandable and part of the frame of reference of the person being interviewed. During to discuss an idea or feeling, and she may then remain in control of the interaction. In other cases, the subject may have no commitment to any one line of discussion, and she may expect the interviewer to lead the conversation.

The conversational mode is probably the least threatening way of conducting interviews. It can be a valuable tool for probing a subject's feelings. At the time of the interview, subjects may not have had time to consider their feelings about an exhibition or program, and when they are confronted by an interviewer who asks their opinion, they may find that they do not really have one. In a conversational interview, however, subjects are able to think about, probe, discuss, and sometimes even test their ideas. They can gain clarity in what their own beliefs are, and this can provide useful insights. This same process of self-exploration, however, has its disadvantages. Some subjects are highly suggestible, and they may quickly incorporate their ideas of what they think the interviewer wants into their own belief system. These subjects may report on what they believe the interviewer wants to hear, instead of relating their own experiences. Other subjects enjoy not having a fixed belief or opinion and frequently change their ideas throughout a conversational interview. Although some subjects require careful monitoring, the informal conversational interview can be a valuable source of ideas and general impressions.

Semi-Structured Interviews

Another kind of interview is called the semi-structured interview. In this method, the interviewer specifies the topics and issues for the interview but leaves open the exact way that the questions will be asked. You may identify a series of topics that need to be covered, but how each question is asked may depend on the circumstances of the particular interview. The semi-structured interview is particularly useful when interviewing children. It may be important to know that the same topics are covered with each child, but not all of them may understand the same words, either because their language abilities are not well developed or because English is not their primary language. This interview technique allows the researcher to substitute words that may be more easily understood, or to ask a question in several different ways.

One form that the semi-structured interview takes is the focus group. Focus groups are comprised of participants who are similar in some specific way, either because of their interests, past experience, or membership in a particular demographic category (e.g., income level or ethnic group). Focus groups are often used to learn about how a target audience might react to a specific product or planned program.

Open-Ended Interviews

In the open-ended interview, the researcher determines the exact questions ahead of time, but not the response categories. Since each subject is asked the same question, you know that variability in the responses is not due to variations in how the questions were presented. This maintains consistency in the data. In addition, since the response categories are not designated in advance, the method allows for unusual or innovative responses. In formative evaluation, open-ended interviews can be helpful in gathering subjects' responses to exhibit models or prototypes. Consistency of questioning is useful, allowing the data to be standardized across a number of subjects, but the wide range of possible visitor responses provides the clearest picture of the strengths and weaknesses of the test exhibits.

Structured Interviews

Of all the interview types, structured interviews lend themselves best to statistical analysis. In interviews of this type, the questions and response categories are determined ahead of time, enabling the findings from large samples of subjects to be summarized and analyzed. As in questionnaires, the form of the questions in a structured interview will greatly influence how a subject responds. As mentioned above, subjects often find it easier to place their opinions in a category rather than to provide a direct answer. If categorical alternatives are given in an interview, provide them in writing on a card so the subjects don't have to memorize them.

A Multicultural Case Study

One of the most comprehensive museum-based interview projects was a multicultural audience study called the Bay Area Research Project (Museum Management Consultants 1994). The authors of the study interviewed a sample of 1,697 adult residents in the San Francisco Bay Area, selecting subjects from random telephone lists that were purchased for each of three nonwhite ethnic groups in the region. The researchers had specific criteria for whom to include (individuals had to be an adult over seventeen years of age, they had to have visited a museum at least once in their life, etc.), and it actually required a total of 15,313 calls to get an acceptable number of respondents. The interview protocol was first tested in advance with a small number of subjects. Then, respondents were interviewed over the phone by trained bilingual interviewers and were offered the option to conduct the interview in English, Spanish, Cantonese, Mandarin, or Tagalog. The interviews included both closed and open-ended questions, as well as questions about the respondents' demographic characteristics. For example, in the following closed question, the interviewers read both the question and the possible answers to the respondent:

Who would you usually go with on a trip to a museum? Would it be . . . ?

1. With a friend
2. With your family
3. With your spouse or partner
4. By yourself
5. With a group

Other questions were asked as open-ended questions, and the interviewer immediately categorized the responses. In the following example, the answers were not read aloud to the subject:

What kinds of things would encourage you to go to a museum more often?

1. Better transportation
2. More exhibits based on your culture
3. Lower entrance fee
4. Available day care
5. More activities for your family
6. Different hours
7. Nothing
8. Free day
9. Something else _____
10. Don't know
11. Refused

Other questions were completely open-ended:

When you think of museums, what is the first thing that comes to mind?

Still other questions included rating scales:

I'm going to read you a list of visitor services or amenities that are found in museums. Please tell me whether the visitor service is very important (4), important (3), somewhat important (2), or not important to you (1).

A. People who can answer your questions	1	2	3	4
B. Information about what is there and how to get around	1	2	3	4
C. Visitor maps and signs	1	2	3	4
D. Information in languages other than English	1	2	3	4

The very last questions, which were necessary for the study, were also the most personal and intrusive:

Which country were you born in?
How long have you lived in this country?
Which country were your parents born in?

Through the use of a wide range of question types, a carefully designed selection procedure, and experienced interviewers, the authors of this study gained a remarkably comprehensive picture of how multicultural audiences experience museums. This type of study can provide the museums of an entire region with information that can help them diversify and expand their audiences.

Projective Measures

Sometimes subjects find it difficult to respond to direct questions. It may be easier for them to answer hypothetical questions about what someone else might think or to describe in a picture what a person might feel. These projective techniques allow subjects literally to *project* their feelings and thoughts onto an imagined situation, picture, or inanimate object. For example, instead of asking a subject what was difficult for her, you can ask, "What do you think other visitors would find difficult?" Lucille Nahemow (1971:91) asked subjects in one museum study, "How would you describe the room to one of your friends?" This can increase a subject's comfort level by putting a little distance between the person and her response.

Similarly, informal researchers have used drawings or photographs to help subjects to imagine the situation that they are asked to discuss. Sherman Rosenfeld (1982) refers to these as "picture-stimulus questions" (figure 11).

Another way to access information from children is to use props. When the prop is a doll, the subject can act out an experience using the doll to represent himself. You can ask the subject to describe what that "child" (the doll) will see, what he will do, and how he feels about those experiences: "What does this doll like to do in the zoo?" Or ask a series of questions: "The teacher says that the doll can visit a few exhibits. Which ones do you think he will choose?" After the choice is made, ask "Why did he choose those?" Young subjects often have an easier time expressing their opinions in the context of a story, rather than as responses to unconnected questions.

Projective measures can be very sensitive, but they also can be variable and easily influenced by any number of factors. Researchers at Girls Incorporated, a national organization that provides programs and career activities for girls, asked subjects to draw a picture of a scientist at work, then to select characteristics that best described their picture (Nicholson et al. 1994). The researchers initially expected to see differences in the children's drawings before and after their program, which was specifically designed to reduce stereotyping of scientists. However, during a second round of testing that included subjects who did not participate in the special program, many more of the girls drew

Figure 11. Images used for picture-stimulus questions at an experimental mini-zoo at the Lawrence Hall of Science. Children were asked to imagine how the child, always the same age and sex as the subject, responded in each situation. In the upper picture, the child is telling friends what he/she liked and disliked. In the lower picture, the child is telling classmates what he/she learned (Rosenfeld 1982:195).

female scientists without an intervening program or activity to encourage a reduction of stereotyping of scientists. The projective measure was sufficiently volatile that the context of the group and the test itself was enough to elicit a change in the responses.

Expert Assessments

Sometimes it is useful to have a group of experts observe your program or exhibits and make recommendations for improvement. Various journals now include critics' reviews of exhibits, much in the same way that critics review films or books; for example, Beverly Gordon (1995) reviewed the Chicago Historical Society exhibit *Becoming American Women: Clothing and the Jewish Immigrant Experience, 1880–1920* for the journal *American Quarterly.*

The most common form of expert assessment is a panel that is assembled to review an exhibit or program. When using expert panels, it is important to give considerable thought to how you choose the panelists. It is helpful to have people who are knowledgeable about informal education practices so they are aware of the constraints present in these environments. The experts should have demonstrated abilities to give critical feedback—a panel of experts who say only that you are doing a good job may boost your morale, but it will not help improve your programs. The panelists should also be sufficiently detached from your day-to-day affairs that they have little invested in the direction that your programs take. There are several good places to look for experts:

- People who have served as grant panelists or who have served as principal investigators for major grants-funded projects in your field. Their names can be obtained from the program officer at foundations and federal agencies.

- Editorial board reviewers for publications in your field.

- Typical users or visitors who have been selected because they are both verbal and can provide critical insight. Sometimes a panel of experts composed of carefully selected children can add considerable insight to a program being evaluated.

In a study in an art museum, Kathryne Andrews (1979) invited a group of twelve high school students to serve on an expert panel. The group of teenagers helped the researchers to interpret data from a questionnaire that had been sent to 520 young adults. The researchers also asked the students about their best and worst experiences with museums, the relationship between school and the museum, their attitudes about the value of visiting museums, and their reactions to unfamiliar art. The teenage experts talked frankly to the researchers about young people's educational priorities and special interests. In this way, a panel of experts not only provided information for the evaluation but also assisted in the data interpretation.

Daryl Fischer (1997) suggests that visitor panels can be useful at different stages in the exhibit-development process. During the preliminary stages of concept development, visitor panels can serve as part of the front-end evaluation, helping staff explore possible approaches to an exhibit or program based on their previous knowledge of the topic. Early in the exhibit-development process, they can assist the formative evaluation, measuring the effectiveness of label prototypes. Once the exhibit is completed, visitor panels can be used as part of the summative evaluation to assess overall effectiveness.

Questionnaire Guidelines

When you ask a subject to respond to written questions on paper or computer, this is usually referred to as a questionnaire. Questionnaires have an advantage over interviews in that they can be given out to subjects without the evaluator being present. And because the evaluator may not be present, she is less likely to have an influence on a subject's responses. However, questionnaires have the disadvantage that there is no way to clarify subjects' answers; subjects may understand a survey question to mean something other than what the researcher intended.

The best way to ensure that your survey questions are clearly understood is to test them beforehand. You may present a draft of your questionnaire to a small sample of subjects and then review them to see if the answers are ambiguous. Time how long it takes for the subjects to fill out the questionnaire, so you can determine whether it is of a reasonable length. It may also be useful to ask the questionnaire items in an interview first, so you can ask the subjects to restate their answers to clarify their intentions. Results from the practice sessions can then be used to rephrase questions to be more effective.

How the language in a questionnaire is phrased will always influence the responses of the subjects. According to Roger Miles and his colleagues,

> The actual words used in a questionnaire are so obviously crucial that it is surprising how often they tend to be phrased in a technical language or assume a particular class-bound mode of expression. Question wording should be free from technical terms (unless, of course, it is written for technical people), unambiguous and to the point. Furthermore, questions should be written in a language that is

acceptable and appropriate to the visitors being interviewed, but this does not mean visitors should be talked down to. The fundamental precept in writing questionnaires is to imagine the people who are going to be asked to answer, and develop questions that are understandable and appropriate to them. (1988: 161)

At the beginning of the questionnaire, briefly tell the purpose of the study and the institutional sponsor. Written informed consent may not be required if your subjects are adults, as long as they know they are free to decline to participate. However, if the questionnaire subjects are children, the disabled, or any other population that is at risk, you should include the full procedures for informed consent (see chapter 3). If a questionnaire is to be mailed to respondents, always include a letter of introduction.

Try to minimize the amount of time it will take for someone to fill out a questionnaire. Generally, the longer it looks like it will take, the fewer people will choose to respond. Try to make the process of filling out the questionnaire an enjoyable experience; it should not feel like taking a test. After all, you are asking the subject to give you something valuable—their time and information. An enjoyable or fun survey can be a reward in itself. For children, making a questionnaire fun can be as simple as including happy and sad faces as options to express their feelings, using a bright color of paper, or placing appropriate little figures in the margins, although it should not be so cluttered that it impairs the child's ability to read or respond. You can also consider more tangible rewards for participating in your study. A free admission ticket, a poster, a logo pin, a pencil, or a reduced rate on a membership can make subjects feel very positive about having given their time.

Ross Loomis emphasizes that it is important to limit the range of questions asked in a survey:

Most surveys suffer from having far too broad a range of questions. This only adds to their superficiality. In anticipating a survey, you should ask: "What is the single most important visitor-related problem facing the museum?" If a survey does nothing more than provide information on that question, it will have some utility. (1973:24)

One of the most common type of questionnaire used in a museum is the demographic survey. These typically ask about the audience's sex, age of children, experience with the institution (e.g., number of times visited), educational background, and interests as they relate to the institution being studied (table 6). Demographic surveys should

Table 6. Examples of questions commonly asked in demographic surveys conducted in informal educational settings.

How many times have you visited before?
How many times have you visited in the past twelve months?
When did you first plan your visit?
Why did you visit today?
How did you learn about (the institution or program)?
How long did you plan to stay for your visit?
Did you have plans to see any particular exhibit or event?
What did you expect to do or see during your visit?
What exhibits did you visit?
What do you remember about the visit that interested you most?
How far do you live from (the institution)?
Where did you park?
Who did you visit with?
What do you do for a living?
What is your educational background?
What is your background in the subject matter of the institution (program)?
To which age grouping do you belong?
To which gender grouping do you belong?

Source: Adapted from McManus 1991 and Museum Management Consultants 1994.

not request personal information such as subjects' income, where they live, or their religious or political affiliation, unless it is imperative for the study. In general, demographic surveys are most accurate when they request factual information about a subject's background or opinions on a topic, and they are least accurate when they request detailed quantitative information (e.g., "How long did you visit the zoo today?" or "How many exhibits did you visit?"). Subjects may have clear ideas about who they are and what they feel, but they are often poor estimators of time and specific quantities.

Sometimes the order in which the responses are presented can influence the subject's choice. Priscilla Salant and Don Dillman (1994) suggest that subjects in mail surveys tend to pick the first answer more often. On the other hand, in telephone or face-to-face interviews, they tend to pick the last. If you think that respondents are choosing the first answer they are presented with, then it might be useful to change the order of the responses. If your choices are, for example, "more," "about the same," or "less," then have each third of the questionnaires use a different first answer.

Whenever possible, phrase your questions to make it as easy as possible for someone to respond. Sometimes it is more trouble to answer a question that is very general. For example, instead of asking, "How much would you spend for your museum visit?" you might ask the question as follows:

About how much money would you spend on the following?

Planetarium show	$_____.00
Educational tour	$_____.00
IMAX theater presentation	$_____.00
Use of audio tour	$_____.00

Use of interactive kit	$_____.00
Entry into discovery room	$_____.00
General admission	$_____.00

Make the survey as easy as possible to return. If you expect subjects to fill out the questionnaire in the museum, provide a comfortable place for them to answer the questions. If your questionnaire is being administered on a computer, make sure you provide seating and a quiet place to respond away from the main flow of traffic. It is generally a poor idea to ask visitors to complete questionnaires as they are entering a museum, because the pressure of the incoming visitor traffic can make the experience stressful. If you expect the subjects to return the questionnaire by mail, include a stamped self-addressed envelope.

As is the case with interviews, if you have to ask personal questions, include them at the end of the questionnaire. Ask the subjects whether they would like to see a report on the findings, and leave space for them to give their name and address so you can reply to them. Be sure to thank the subjects for their time. Examples of some brief questionnaires are shown in figures 12 and 13.

Writing Questions

Questionnaires, like interviews, can be qualitative or quantitative. A qualitative approach to a questionnaire is open-ended: the subjects can respond to the questions in their own manner, generating their own ideas in their own words. Subjects may be asked to generate their own questions, or they may be given the opportunity to respond by drawing pictures. One questionnaire contained a single item on a mostly blank but brightly colored page: "What do you want to tell us about our library?"

What's In the Water?

Discovery Day
Adults: TELL US WHAT YOU THINK!

Name: _____

1. How was the Discovery Day for you? Check one.

    ☐ Bad   ☐ Okay   ☐ Good   ☐ Great

2. How was the Discovery Day for the girl(s) you came with?

    ☐ Bad   ☐ Okay   ☐ Good   ☐ Great

3. Check how you felt about:
    Location of Discovery Day ☐ Easy to get here   ☐ Hard to get here

    Length of Discovery Day ☐ Too short   ☐ Just right   ☐ Too long

4. Do you want to come to another GAC Discovery Day?   Check one.

    ☐ I will definitely come.
    ☐ I will try to come.
    ☐ I am not sure.
    ☐ I do not think I'll come.

    Why? _____

5. What did you like most about this Discovery Day? Why?

    _____

    _____

    _____

6. What did you learn about the girl(s) you brought today?

    _____

    _____

    _____

DD2/End/Adults/Pink/   ⟶

Figure 12. A questionnaire developed by the Institute for Learning Innovation, Annapolis, for the program Girls at the Center at The Franklin Institute Science Museum and the Girl Scouts of the U.S.A. (McCreedy 1997).

7. **Was there something we should have done differently? If yes, what?**

_____

_____

_____

8. **Is this your first GAC event?**   ☐ Yes   ☐ No
    If not, what other GAC events have you attended?
    ☐ Sneak Preview Workshop   ☐ Discovery Day   ☐ Family ScienceFest
    ☐ Other _____

9. **Why did you come today?** _____

In order to be sure we are including people from many backgrounds, we ask that you answer the following questions.

Are you: ☐ American Indian/Alaskan Native   ☐ Asian/Pacific Islander
            ☐ African American/Black   ☐ White   ☐ Other race/Multiracial

Are you also Hispanic/Latino?   ☐ Yes   ☐ No

Are you involved in Girl Scouts?   ☐ Yes   ☐ No
    If yes, in what way? _____

Is this your first visit to this museum?   ☐ Yes   ☐ No
    If not, how many times have you been here before? _____

Name of the girl you brought: _____   Her age: ___
Is she: ☐ American Indian/Alaskan Native   ☐ Asian/Pacific Islander
           ☐ African American/Black   ☐ White   ☐ Other race/Multiracial

Is she also Hispanic/Latino?   ☐ Yes   ☐ No
Her relationship to you: (example: daughter) _____

Anything else you want to tell us? _____

Figure 12, continued.

SESSION EVALUATION FORM
1994 AAM Annual Meeting, Seattle, Washington

Session:_____ Date:_____ Time:_____

Please circle the number that best represents your feeling about the speakers and overall session.

Speaker   Ratings

Session Chair:_____

Organized	6	5	4	3	2	1	Disorganized
Interesting	6	5	4	3	2	1	Dull
Valuable	6	5	4	3	2	1	Useless
Overall Excellent	6	5	4	3	2	1	Overall unsatisfactory

Speaker:_____

Organized	6	5	4	3	2	1	Disorganized
Interesting	6	5	4	3	2	1	Dull
Valuable	6	5	4	3	2	1	Useless
Overall Excellent	6	5	4	3	2	1	Overall unsatisfactory

Speaker:_____

Organized	6	5	4	3	2	1	Disorganized
Interesting	6	5	4	3	2	1	Dull
Valuable	6	5	4	3	2	1	Useless
Overall Excellent	6	5	4	3	2	1	Overall unsatisfactory

Speaker:_____

Organized	6	5	4	3	2	1	Disorganized
Interesting	6	5	4	3	2	1	Dull
Valuable	6	5	4	3	2	1	Useless
Overall Excellent	6	5	4	3	2	1	Overall unsatisfactory

Session   Rating

Overall Excellent	6	5	4	3	2	1	Overall unsatisfactory

Did the Annual Meeting Program accurately describe the content that was covered in this session?   _____Yes   _____No

Did the session address current issues?   _____Yes   _____No

Additional Comments and suggestions for future programs, etc. (use other side if necessary):

Figure 13. A questionnaire developed by the staff of the American Association of Museums for its 1994 annual meeting. Participants were asked to rate the quality of each session.

Quantitative approaches to questionnaires tend to be more structured. The questions may include various choices for answers, so that the responses can be categorized effectively. Some questionnaires will include a rating scale listing numbers from one to three or one to five, with each number symbolizing a value:

What were you interested in during high school?
(Circle your response to each)

	Not at all	Some		Very Much	
People or friends	1	2	3	4	5
Sports	1	2	3	4	5
Science or math or technology	1	2	3	4	5
Politics or social issues	1	2	3	4	5
Art or music or theater	1	2	3	4	5
Reading or literature	1	2	3	4	5
Other_____	1	2	3	4	5

There are many ways to phrase the questions and responses. Below are various examples of ways to ask someone's opinion:

Is _____better, worse, or the same as _____?

1. Much better
2. Somewhat better
3. Same
4. Somewhat worse
5. Much worse

To what extent do you agree or disagree with the statement, _____?

1. Strongly disagree
2. Somewhat disagree
3. Neither disagree nor agree
4. Somewhat agree
5. Strongly agree

How would you rate _____?

1. Lower than low
2. Low
3. Medium
4. High
5. Perfection

Circle the number that best represents your feelings about_____?

Well Organized	6	5	4	3	2	1	Disorganized
Interesting	6	5	4	3	2	1	Boring
Valuable	6	5	4	3	2	1	Worthless
Excellent	6	5	4	3	2	1	Poor

Please rate how useful this program was for you?

1. Not at all useful
2. Somewhat useful
3. Very useful

How important is it to you to _____?

1. Very important
2. Somewhat important
3. Little importance
4. Not needed

Sometimes subjects choose the neutral value more often. If this is a concern, the scale can be designed to run from one to four, so there is no middle choice. It is also useful to include a "no answer" (NA) option for subjects who may not be informed enough to voice an opinion and an "other" option for subjects who might want to present alternative answers.

The largest difference between qualitative and quantitative approaches to questionnaires is how the results are presented. For qualitative questions, the researcher summarizes general trends in narrative form, giving verbatim examples of different responses to show variability. In quantitative questions, the results are categorized, described, and often analyzed using statistical tests. Combining qualitative and quantitative approaches in the same questionnaire is an effective way to uncover general trends while gaining insight into individual differences. Figures 14 and 15 show examples of questionnaires that combine quantitative and qualitative approaches.

N E B R A S K A
MATH & SCIENCE
INITIATIVE

Academic Year 1996-97

Dear Nebraska Teacher:

We would like to ask your help in evaluating the Wonderwise Kit you have just learned about.

Administrative Offices

126 North 11th Street
P.O. Box 880231
Lincoln, NE 68588-0231
phone: 402/472-8965
fax: 402/472-9311
e-mail: nmsi@unlinfo.unl.edu

Attached is a brief questionnaire asking what you think about the kit and how useful you think it will be. This should take about ten to twenty minutes for you to complete. Your responses will help us understand how teachers will use these kits and provide important information for future museum projects of this kind. When you are finished, return your completed questionnaire to your workshop leader.

Your responses to this questionnaire will be kept confidential within the project, and no reports published as a result of this evaluation will include any individually identifying information. You are free to decide not to participate in this study or to withdraw at any time without adversely affecting your relationship with the investigators or the University of Nebraska. Your decision will not result in any loss of benefits to which you are otherwise entitled.

K-12 Project

126 Morrill Hall
University of Nebraska-Lincoln
Lincoln, NE 68588-0350
phone: 402/472-9305
fax: 402/472-0932

This evaluation study has received the approval of the University of Nebraska-Lincoln Institutional Review Board (IRB Approval Number 96-06-365). You indicate your consent to participate in the evaluation study by completing and returning the survey. If you have any questions, please contact me or IRB directly at 402-472-6965.

Thank you for your help in this evaluation.

Sincerely,

Amy N. Spiegel
Program Evaluator
Phone: 402-472-0764
email: aspiegel@unlinfo.unl.edu

Figure 14. A letter and questionnaire given to teachers for feedback on the Wonderwise Women in Science kits developed at the University of Nebraska State Museum. The letter both introduces teachers to the questionnaire and serves to obtain informed consent. Teachers are informed of their right not to participate in the study and are told that filling out the questionnaire will indicate their consent. The letter and survey were given to teachers who attended workshops and/or institutes on the Wonderwise project (Spiegel and Dethlefs 1997).

Wonderwise Kits in the Classroom

Today's Date _____   Name of your school _____

ESU # (to which your district belongs) _____   District Name _____

Grade level(s) you are currently teaching: 2 3 4 5 6 7 8
(circle all that apply)

1) Please circle the components of each kit that you learned about today:

Sea Otter Kit	Pollen Kit	Parasitology Kit	Rainforest Kit	Plants and People Kit
Video	Video	Video	Video	Video
Activity Book	Activity Book	Activity Book	Activity Book	Activity Book
Biography	Biography	Biography	Biography	Biography
CD-ROM		CD-ROM	CD-ROM	

Video

2) Do you anticipate being able to use the video(s) in your classroom teaching? (Circle one)

Definitely WOULD NOT use   Probably not   Maybe   Probably   Definitely WOULD use

3) If not, why not?

4) Was the video on target for the grade level you teach?

Too simplistic   About right   Too complex

5) Was the video about the right length for the topic presented?

Too short   About the right length   Too long

6) How well would the video fit into the science units you teach?

Would be difficult to include   Could be worked into units   Would fit into units very well

Activity Book

7) Will these activities be useful to you in your classroom? (Circle one)

Not at all useful   Somewhat useful   Very useful

8) Do you think these activities will engage your students?

Not at all engaging   Somewhat engaging   Very engaging

9) How well do you think these activities fit into the state science framework?

Not at all well   Somewhat   Very well   Not familiar with framework

10) How well would these activities fit in with the units of study you are already teaching?

Not at all well   Somewhat   Very well

11) To what extent do you think these activities impart a general theme of scientific inquiry?

Not at all   Somewhat   Very much

12) How easy do you think the activities will be for you to use? (circle one)

Difficult to use   With considerable work, could use   With normal preparation, easy to use

Figure 14, continued.

Biography

13) Do you anticipate being able to use this written biography in your classroom teaching?

Definitely WOULD NOT use	Probably not	Maybe	Probably	Definitel WOULI use

14) If not, why not?

15) If yes, how do you anticipate using this biography? (Check all that apply)

_____ As part of science class

_____ As part of reading/literature class

_____ To help integrate reading and science

_____ Other (please describe) _____

CD-ROM

16) How do you anticipate using the CD-ROM with your students? (check all that apply)

[_____ I do not have access to a CD-ROM machine, so I will not use the CD-ROM]

_____ As a follow-up activity for students to pursue on their own

_____ As part of a unit that engages the whole class

_____ For students to view the video individually

_____ For students to use an optional resource

_____ Other, please explain _____

_____

The Wonderwise Kits

17) How effective do you think these kits will be in getting your students more interested in science? (Circle one)

Not at all effective	Somewhat effective	Very effective

18) Why?

19) How effective do you think these kits will be in getting **girls** more interested in science?

Not at all effective	Somewhat effective	Very effective

20) Why?

21) If you have any additional comments, particularly about the strengths and weaknesses of these kits, please feel free to write on the back of this page.

Thank you very much for your valuable input!

Figure 14, continued.

exploratorium

3601 Lyon Street
San Francisco,
California 94123
(415) 563-7337

Dear Former Explainer:

As a former explainer at the Exploratorium, you are part of a large
and diverse extended family. Your members number almost 1,000,
work in many fields, and live throughout the world, from San
Francisco to South Africa to Nepal.

Over the past four months, we have been tracking you down, by
methods both direct and roundabout. Some of you were a quick
phone call away; others we found through the grapevine. The
purpose of our search for addresses and phones has been to re-
establish contact and to send you the enclosed questionnaire.

The questionnaire is an opportunity for us to better understand
the impact of the explainer program on you, the explainers, and
to find ways to improve the program. We hope you will fill out
the questionnaire and return it to us as soon as possible in the
enclosed stamped envelope. It should take you about 10-20 minutes
to complete the questionnaire. We hope it brings back good memories
and inspires you to visit us next time you're in the area. Please call
us at the above number if you have any questions. We thank you
ahead of time for your help.

Sincerely,

Judy Diamond and Beth Cleary
Explainer Survey Staff

*Figure 15. A questionnaire sent from the Exploratorium to its former Explainers. It was
used, along with in-depth interviews, to assess the long-term impacts of the program
(from Diamond et al. 1987).*

REMEMBER BACK WHEN YOU WERE AN EXPLAINER?
What was it like? From the first day to the last, what stands out
for you? (Please continue on the back or attach paper if necessary)

1. Explaining: What do you remember about learning to explain?
    What stands out about your experiences of communicating with
    other people, conveying a message and/or teaching?

2. Your Relationship with People: Looking back, what do you
    remember about relating to the other explainers and/or
    the public? What did you learn about working with people?

3. Learning: How did you learn the science you were explaining?
    Did you learn from the staff, from other explainers, and/or on
    your own from the exhibits? Did you learn anything about
    learning?

Figure 15, continued.

4. AFTER YOU STOPPED WORKING IN THE EXPLORATORIUM: We'd like to know what ways being an explainer affected your life. To what extent did the Explainer Program have impact on you? (Circle your response to each.)

Did your experience with the Explainer Program increase any of the following:	No Impact		Some Impact		Lots of Impact
Your self-confidence	1	2	3	4	5
Your understanding of your capabilities	1	2	3	4	5
Your desire to learn on your own	1	2	3	4	5
Your curiosity about how things work	1	2	3	4	5
Your desire to work with people	1	2	3	4	5
Your ability to teach people	1	2	3	4	5
Your effectiveness in other jobs	1	2	3	4	5
Your intention to go to college or other school after high school	1	2	3	4	5
Your interest in art	1	2	3	4	5
Your interest in science	1	2	3	4	5
Your confidence that you could understand science	1	2	3	4	5
The amount you read about science or scientists	1	2	3	4	5
The number of science courses you took or plan to take in school or college	1	2	3	4	5
The amount you watch science programs on TV or listen to them on the radio	1	2	3	4	5
Other_____	1	2	3	4	5

5. Are there other ways that working as an explainer affected you or had impact on your life? (Please answer on the back.)

Figure 15, continued.

6. What year(s) and term(s) did you work as an explainer?
   plainer?_____

7. What school were you going to when you first started as an
   explainer? _____

8. What were you interested in during high school? (Circle your
   response to each)

	Not at All		Some		Very Much
People or friends	1	2	3	4	5
Sports	1	2	3	4	5
Science or math or technology	1	2	3	4	5
Politics or social issues	1	2	3	4	5
Art or music or theatre	1	2	3	4	5
Reading or literature	1	2	3	4	5
Other_____	1	2	3	4	5

9. What is the highest grade that you completed in school?
   (Circle one)

   High School   College or Technical School   Post-College
   1 2 3 4   1 2 3 4   1 2 3 4+

   If you went to (or are now in) college or technical school,
   what did you major in?_____

   If you went to (or are now in) school after college, what did
   you study? _____

10. Did you work in other jobs at the Exploratorium during or
    after your work as an Explainer? _____ Yes _____ No
                   If Yes, what did you do?_____

11. What kind of work are you doing now (what is your job)?_____
12. What is your ethnic origin? ____Black ____Hispanic
    ____Caucasian ____Chinese ____Asian (not Chinese)
    ____Other_____

13. What is your sex? ____Female ____Male

NAME_____
Street_____
City_____State_____Zip Code_____
Phone_____

                   THANK YOU FOR YOUR HELP.

Figure 15, continued.

Chapter 6

Measuring Learning

Informal educational settings provide experiences that are diverse and generally unpredictable. Visitors spend their time observing, reading, playing, interacting socially, sometimes attending to personal needs, and often interacting with stimuli in the environment. Visitors observe the phenomena displayed in exhibits, the actions of other visitors, demonstrations, and other kinds of presentations. They interact with the environment by manipulating exhibits, moving through spaces, and socializing with other people. They sometimes spend time reading—instructions, labels, signs, or brochures. I have even observed visitors sitting in museums reading books that they have brought with them.

In informal settings, however, people rarely spend time reflecting upon or synthesizing their experiences. As Jeremy Roschelle (1995) has pointed out, conceptual change is unlikely to occur within a single visit. It may take days, weeks, or months for the informal educational experience to be integrated sufficiently with prior knowledge for significant learning to be measurable. This provides a special challenge when we attempt to measure learning in informal settings. Although visitors may have experienced a great deal, they often take days or weeks to integrate their new experiences into a conceptual framework; within shorter time frames, they may not be aware of any learning having occurred.

Pre- and Post- Measures

One common way to tell the effect of an exhibit or program is to measure some aspect of a visitor's knowledge or behavior before he or she experiences the activity and then remeasure the same variable afterward. The variable to be tested for differences should be one that is likely to be influenced by the exhibit or program. Typically, students are given a test of some sort before they go into the exhibit, and then they are retested after they leave that particular gallery. Differences in the two tests may be attributed to the effects of the exhibit.

In the freewheeling informal environment, pre- and posttests (or posttest-only designs) present special challenges. Since visitors aren't necessarily directed to pay attention to specific elements, it is not obvious which features of the environment one should test. Invariably, when a pretest is introduced into this environment, it signals the users to pay particular attention to the variables the test contains. The results of the pre- and posttest may suggest impacts of the gallery, but these impacts may only be relevant for the condition of the test, when users are directed to particular aspects of the exhibit.

An alternative method is a posttest-only design, in which subjects randomly assigned to each of two groups are compared on their test performance after exposure to the exhibit or program. This avoids the problem of sensitizing the pretest subjects to the material likely to be tested. Posttest-only designs have their problems, however, since they assume that all of the subjects will be exposed to the same features of the environment. Since informal environments involve a free choice of features, it is not typical for everyone to see or do the same thing. These experimental designs are less likely to provide information on what the typical visitor learns in the museum, zoo, or park, as to inform us about what visitors are capable of learning, when they are so directed.

One can sometimes arrange for a control group or a comparison group. Using a control or comparison group does not ameliorate the influence of the pretest, but it increases the validity of the experiment. In these cases, subjects are randomly assigned to one or more experimental groups or to the control group. Each experimental group is given the pretest. Each may, for example, be exposed to a different tour format, such as a lecture-based tour versus a participatory tour. The control group is not exposed to the tour; instead, it may be allowed to roam freely through the museum. Then all groups are given the posttest. Measurement of the differences between the tests in the groups can provide insight into which kind of tour or free time was most effective at teaching the concepts measured on the test.

A general rule for this model is to make the pretest and posttest questions realistic indicators of what people are expected to learn in a museum. For example, they should not rely heavily on detailed factual information that might be contained in exhibit labels. Rather, the questions should ask about the subject's experience with or attitudes toward the phenomena demonstrated by the exhibits. Thus you might ask: "How does your experience with this exhibit relate to anything you have done outside the museum? What kinds of questions does this particular exhibit make you think of? How does this exhibit relate to books, videos, or other resources you know of? What would you tell a child about the exhibit you have just seen?"

Pretests and posttests should be used cautiously in informal settings since conceptual change in informal settings is often very gradual. If the pretest and posttest occur within a few hours of one another, it may be too short a time to measure the kinds of learning that occur. If they occur several days or weeks after one another, it may be too long a time, and information and experiences may be forgotten. In general, the pretest and posttest model tends to de-emphasize more significant informal learning experiences in favor of simple kinds of text-based information.

Measuring Recall and Recognition

There are many dimensions to human memory, but one of the most readily understood is the distinction between recall and recognition. Recall is the memory capacity used in quiz shows: The contestant is given a bare minimum of information to cue the answer, and he must search for the correct word or concept that fits the data supplied. Recognition is the memory used in finding your way around a neighborhood that you haven't visited in a long time. Certain views will trigger a sense of familiarity, of having seen them before, and by following a trail of familiar sights, you can navigate through the area.

In informal learning environments, where visitors are exposed to an enormous amount of different kinds of information, it is relatively difficult to test for recall. Visitors typically wander through a museum making their own decisions about what to pay attention to. As mentioned earlier, Frank Oppenheimer (1972) likens this to sightseeing, where tourists visit a complex environment and select items of interest. Unless one devises ways to change the nature of the informal environment by structuring the learning experiences, there is no reason to expect that a typical visitor should be able to recall specific information. There are only a few natural conditions with enough structure to make the measurement of recall an appropriate methodology for informal learning environments. For example, you might expect to find high levels of recall under the following conditions:

- The researcher first observes the subject interacting with a specific exhibit, and the subject manipulates the exhibit correctly, reads the labels aloud, or makes a specific comment that refers to the content of a label.

- The subjects are staff or volunteers who have been trained specifically to help the public understand the exhibits, who have been given tours or who have attended programs that emphasize the content of the exhibit.

- The researcher establishes an experiment in which subjects are asked to read a label and/or interact with an exhibit, then asks the subject the meaning of what is presented.

Marty Klein (1981) suggests that the recognition of information is a more sensitive measure of retention and is more easily elicited. Recognition is also more easily measured in informal learning environments, although it, too, has limitations. Sighted visitors store vast amounts of information as visual images that are collected as they wander through a museum. The most useful recognition tests, therefore, are visually based and measure what subjects remember having seen during a visit. Recognition tests that require reading are the less-preferred mode for informal learning environments.

Text-based information presented in labels may be read only by some kinds of visitors. For example, in family groups it is more common for an adult, particularly an adult female, to read the labels (Diamond 1980, 1986; McManus 1989a, 1989b). These are frequently read aloud to other members of the group, with the result that children, in particular, usually hear labels rather than read them. Therefore the best tests of recognition of text-based information may be those in which the text is read aloud to the subjects.

Questions can be designed to measure either recall or recognition. Roger Miles and his colleagues (1988) point out that recognition plays a role in cued retrieval of information, such as is required in multiple-choice tests. Recall memory plays a role in short-answer or fill-in-the-blank tests. The following examples show how questions can be written to measure either recall or recognition:

Questions that test recall:

What is a dinosaur? _____
A dinosaur is _____
Define dinosaur. _____

Question that tests recognition:

Check which of the following is true of dinosaurs:
1. Reptiles
2. Extinct
3. A kind of animal
4. Amphibians
5. Living today

Another possibility is to have the subjects look at pictures or models of different kinds of animals. Each subject is then asked to sort the dinosaurs from the animals that are not. It is very helpful to clarify the subject's answer by asking, "Why?" after they tell you which picture or model is a dinosaur.

If multiple choice answers are too obvious and easy, subjects will be able to figure them out without the help of the museum or zoo experience. If they are too detailed and difficult, no amount of label reading and exhibit interaction will help the subjects answer the questions. The choices need to be appropriate for the type of institution and for the age-level of the audience being tested. Roger Miles points out,

The weakest aspect of multiple-choice forms is the
difficulty in constructing good items. Often the
correct answer can be guessed fairly easily because the
distracters are so obviously wrong. Writing good
items is a creative task ... Usually, when constructing
an objective test, a large list of items is produced
initially, and eliminating the items that are ambiguous
and also those that do not discriminate between
individuals reduces this. Trying out the initial test
items on a sample of visitors for whom the test is
intended does this. (Miles 1988:163)

Children's explanations can also be rated to measure
recall. Joyce Brooks and Philip Vernon (1956) observed students' use of museum exhibits and then interviewed the
children, asking them to name their favorite exhibits. The
subjects chose three exhibits and explained how they
worked. The answers were scored according to the following criteria:

+2 fairly good conception
+1 some conception
 0 don't know
-1 confused
-2 very confused

This technique proved to be a useful way to assess how well
the exhibits were understood by the children.

The Clinical Interview

The Swiss biologist Jean Piaget provided detailed descriptions of how internal mental processes change as a result of
an individual's experience with the world (Piaget 1973,
Piaget and Inhelder 1969). Piaget believed that learning
occurs through the development of schemata in relation to

new experiences. He developed a form of interview called the task-based clinical interview, in which subjects interact with objects and are asked detailed questions about their understanding of those objects. According to Edith Ackerman, a former collaborator of Piaget's in Geneva,

> The clinician's first job is usually to design an experiment that is both conceptually rich and meaningful to the child. The clinician tries to create a "microworld" that embodies and thus reveals the concepts s/he wants to study, and that includes a problem the child is truly interested in tackling— a problem in which the child gets deeply involved. Once the task is designed, the clinician leads the child through the problem, while being guided by the child's own approach. (1988:10)

Ackerman points out that it is easier to emphasize what researchers should not do. They should never try to suggest the right answers to the child, and they should not compare the child's performance to those who might come up with answers that are more similar to an adult's performance. The purpose is not to define a correct or incorrect method for solving the problem:

> The purpose of the clinician is to uncover the originality of the child's reasoning, to rigorously describe its coherence, and to probe its robustness or fragility in a variety of contexts. (1988:10)

This interview technique has been used by Elsa Feher to examine how children acquire an understanding of concepts that are demonstrated in museums (Feher 1990; Feher and Rice 1985; Feher and Meyer 1992; Rice and Feher 1987). Generally, a small number of in-depth interviews constitute the data. According to Feher,

The interviewer, much like an anthropologist in the field, stations herself at the chosen exhibit. When a child approaches and starts investigating the exhibit, the interviewer engages the child in dialogue using questions from a protocol. The protocol is developed from a large number of preliminary test interviews to ensure that the wording, content, and sequencing of the questions yield the best possible information. The questions ask for predictions and explanations of the phenomena that occur when the subject carries out specified tasks at the exhibit, e.g. "What will happen if you do such and such?" and "How can you explain what happened? Can you draw it?"

The intuitive notions that the researchers collect are not simply ad hoc postulates advanced by the children to explain an isolated event. They are ideas organized into full-fledged models that allow for consistent predictions across several different tasks. (1990:37)

To gain access to what Ackerman (1988) calls "deep theories," the clinician varies the constraints of the situation and then invites the subject to make guesses (What do you think will happen?). The subject is asked to express the guesses in various ways, then to probe the guesses experimentally (Let's try . . .). The subject is asked to explain why a given guess was confirmed or not (What actually happened? Did you expect this to happen?), then to propose counter suggestions. The child may then be asked to explain her views, sometimes to another child.

Feher and Meyer (1992) used an exhibit about light to probe children's theories about color. One exhibit, called Street Lights, consists of different types of lamps used in street illumination, including a low-pressure sodium lamp and an incandescent lamp. Visitors can pick up colored objects, walk under the lights, and notice the variation in the objects' apparent color. Because the sodium lamp emits only yellow light, any object held under it will be seen as yellow if its pigments reflect yellow light, or it will look black if its pigments absorb yellow light. The other exhibit, called Primary Lights, consists of a small, darkened room with red, green, and blue lights opposite a large white screen. The visitor can control the lights, turning them off or on independently, and then observe the effects of mixing the colored light in various ways.

In Feher and Meyer's study, using the Street Lights exhibit, they asked eight- to thirteen-year-old subjects to look through a diffraction grating first at a white light and then at the sodium light. The subjects were then asked to look at the colors in some drawings under the white light and to predict what they would look like under the sodium lamp. Finally, the children were asked to take crayons, write their name in various colors, then to predict what their names would look like under the two different kinds of light. The Primary Lights exhibit was then used to explore the children's explanations further. The authors proceeded through a series of questions, asking the children for their predictions, then letting the children produce an effect with the exhibit. If the effect did not match the children's predictions, they were asked to provide an explanation. It is these explanations that provide the material from which Feher and Meyer modeled the children's fundamental understanding and the mental rules that they used for explaining how things worked (table 7). When used with interactive exhibits, the clinical interview thus becomes a powerful tool for understanding how people think in informal educational settings.

Cognitive Maps

Not all of the information that people store in their minds is coded as words. Cognitive maps refer to the way a person's brain represents or stores certain visual information. While the pictures stored are not necessarily correct ones, they guide how people move through environments, how they choose new stimuli, and ultimately how they process new

Table 7. Results of a clinical interview used as a means of eliciting children's understanding of the phenomena shown in exhibits at the Reuben Fleet Space Theater and Science Center. Subjects aged eight to thirteen were interviewed at the exhibit Primary Lights, which consisted of a small, dark room with a red, green, and white light opposite a large white screen (the original version of this exhibit had a blue filter on the white light; this was removed during the interviews). Subjects were asked to explain the effects of blocking the various lights with a tennis ball. In one part of the study, the children were told, "Hold this ball here (between the light and the screen). If I turn on this red light, what will you see on the screen?" This table shows the frequency of responses to the subjects' predictions of the exercise's result. (n=34.)

Type	Example responses	Frequency
The shadow is dark or black	"The light is hitting it [ball] and the shadow will hit the screen and it will be dark."	59%
	"When the light is hitting the ball it [light] doesn't make any color, the ball makes the shadow."	
	"The ball stops the light, it's not the color red anymore and the shadow goes to the wall."	
	"It'll be dark, black because it [ball] is blocking the light."	
The shadow is the color of the light.	"The light is red and it's reflecting off the ball. It is bouncing off the ball."	35%
	"With red light the shadow is red; when you're outside the shadow looks black because the sun's hitting it instead of red."	
The shadow is the color of the object	"Green because the tennis ball is green."	6%

Source: Feher and Meyer 1992:514.

experiences mentally. Ervin Lazlo and his colleagues offer this description of mental maps:

> Cognitive maps are mental representations of the worlds in which we live. They are built of our individual experience, recorded as memories and tested against the unceasing demands of reality. These maps, however, do not simply represent the worlds of our experience in a passive and unchanging way. They are, in fact, dynamic models of the environments in which we carry out our daily lives, and as such determine much of what we expect, and even what we see. Thus, they represent and at the same time participate in the creation of our individual realities. (1996: 3)

First described by the psychologist Edward Tolman in the 1940s, cognitive maps have become a tool in understanding the relationship between an organism and its environment. According to Charles Gallistel (1990), a cognitive map is a record within the central nervous system of macroscopic geometric relations among surfaces in the environment and is used to plan movements through the environment. The relationship between the record in the nervous system and a person's movements may be anything but literal. Herbert Pick (1993) emphasizes that even children may have complex configurational knowledge that guides their movements. For example, children have been shown to reconstruct spatial layouts more accurately if they had walked around the periphery of a space than if they had just walked within the space. They were most accurate when they had walked within the space and their attention was called to the spatial relations.

How children form pictorial representations can help us understand how they may form cognitive maps. Michael Tye (1993) considers three hypotheses for how children form mental pictures: they form *literal* pictures of images,

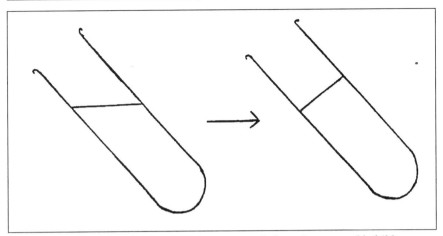

Figure 16. In a series of experiments by Zenon Pylyshyn, four-year-old children were shown an inclined beaker containing a colored liquid (shown at left). When later asked to draw what they had seen, they usually drew the liquid perpendicular to the sides of the beaker, shown at right (Tye 1990:360).

they store fuzzy pictures, and they generate an inner description from concepts that they possess. He considers a series of experiments conducted by Zenon Pylyshyn in which children are shown an inclined beaker. When four-year-old children were shown an inclined beaker containing a colored liquid and are later asked to draw what they saw, they usually drew the fluid level perpendicular to the sides of the beaker, instead of perpendicular to the pull of gravity (figure 16).

If children form literal pictures of their images, there is no reason why they would consistently misrepresent the level of the liquid, but not other elements of the image. If they form fuzzy pictures, there is no reason why the level should always be the fuzzy element—why they would not, for example, draw the beaker incorrectly. The experimenters argue that since children lack the concept of "geometric level" they are unable to draw the picture in the same manner as an adult. They resort instead to a concept they are familiar with: that liquid in cups and pots usually is at right angles to the sides of the container.

In this way, a cognitive map may be like a pictorial representation. Spatial elements that are understandable and thus familiar in some sense may be presented on the map. Elements that are unfamiliar may be distorted, omitted, or translated in some manner. The cognitive map thus encodes a person's understanding and familiarity with an environment, leaving gaps for images that are not understood.

The way that we remember the route to a place is not exactly the same as it is represented in a physical map. We might remember key items at particular locations, such as a stop sign at a corner, a large church, or a park, then use these items to guide our recall of how to navigate there. Large-scale features are used to set a course that brings us into the vicinity of a sought-for place, and then our attention may be shifted to local cues. The way people (and other animals) respond to the spatial configurations of a familiar environment is generally based not on immediate sensory input from the environment but rather on their internal map and their perceived position on the map.

First-time visitors to a museum or zoo create an internal representation of that experience; subsequent visits will lead them to modify the internal representation. How visitors explore the environment, however, and what they ultimately pay attention to, will be largely guided by the internal map. The way people configure a cognitive map can provide clues to the features of the environment that are important, and that may ultimately have resilience in memory. A person's later drawings of the exhibit, room, or museum can yield clues to the meaning of that experience for the individual (figure 17), providing a means for accessing visual memories without first having to rely on verbal reporting of them. When possible, subjects should include verbal descriptions of their drawings to explain features that may not be apparent.

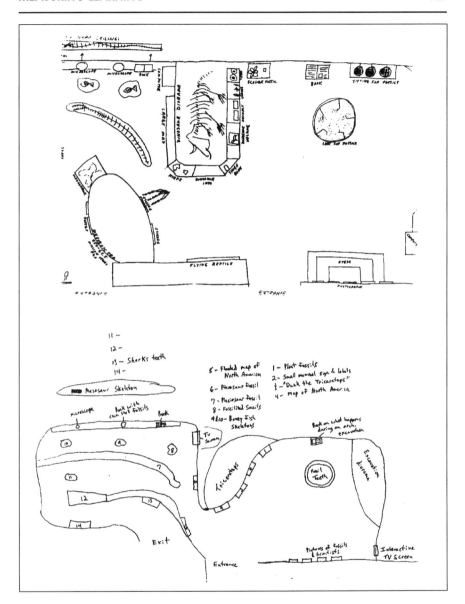

Figure 17. Graduate students were asked to spend thirty minutes visiting the Mesozoic Gallery at the University of Nebraska State Museum. Later, they were asked to draw the gallery and interpret their drawing for the other students. These two drawings show variations in how the students chose to represent the gallery.

One needs to be cautious in interpreting cognitive maps, and the subject's verbal interpretations are as important as actual drawings. Maps are not fixed features, so they may change dramatically from one time to the next. More important experiences may be represented larger than life, or in greater detail than other events, but this is not always so. Finally, subjects vary in their ability to produce various kinds of memory maps. In fact, subjects who have been trained to draw may rely to a greater extent on preexisting rules for re-creating visual scenes, and to a lesser extent on their mental images.

Task Analysis

Sometimes it is useful to ask subjects to recall *exactly* how they performed a task or engaged in an activity. Eliciting this kind of information is not a simple process because many subjects do not know how to remember that much detail. Researchers, however, have used task analysis as a way of gathering details on the cognitive processes involved in physical tasks. This method is a feature of information-processing psychology, and its goal is to uncover how people think while doing complex tasks. In museums, zoos, and parks, this method can be a useful tool for understanding how best to present directions and concepts. Sometimes visitors find a task incomprehensible despite the best efforts to convey it clearly and simply. Information-processing psychology can give insights into how visitors solve problems and why they make errors.

According to Jill Larkin and Barbara Rainard, the procedure begins when a subject is simply asked to do a task and to talk aloud about all thoughts that occur. These comments are tape-recorded and transcribed to a formal record called a protocol.

> A protocol is simply a list of verbal statements made by the problem solver. A protocol is not a complete record of the solver's thoughts nor does it tell why the solver does what he does. The solver does not mention every thought that goes through his head, and protocol statements rarely show why the solver does something. The protocol just provides regular indications of what the solver is thinking. From them the researcher must infer a more complete model of the entire problem solving process. (1984:236)

When a protocol is complete, the next step is to build a process model of the task. The process model includes the representation of the subject's knowledge about the problem, the rules that describe what the subject does as he develops the problem representation, and an interpreter who matches the conditions of the rules against the problem representation. The interpreter produces a series of condition-action rules for building problem representations. Each rule describes an action, together with the conditions under which it is possible and useful to use this action. Each action is a change in the problem representation. When these condition-action rules are then written into a computer program, it becomes a way of testing the problem representation. The computer program verifies whether the condition-action rules are sufficient to solve the problem of interest. In this way, according to Larkin and Rainard, the model solutions are compared to the human solutions to show whether the model provides a good account of what human solvers do.

Jill Larkin used task analysis to model how subjects solve problems that involve everyday tasks. In one study, she modeled the cognitive processes involved in making a cup of coffee (Larkin 1989). Invariably, even simple tasks are much more complicated than one might expect. Larkin identified a total of eighteen subtasks that are required to brew coffee from beans.

A detailed record of the steps involved in performing a task or solving a problem can be a useful guide for informal educational environments. Exhibits frequently have written labels that direct visitors' actions to perform a task and instruct them to observe some effect or change. What might at first appear to be a simple series of actions is not always so, and a task analysis can provide an accurate description of the required steps. Larkin and Rainard (1984) emphasize that the techniques of information-processing psychology are most useful where it is important not just whether individuals can do a certain task, but how they do it.

Chapter 7

Presenting and Analyzing Data

If you have collected quantitative or numerical data, the analysis most often will involve the use of graphs, tables, and statistical techniques to summarize and describe your data. If you collected qualitative data, then the analysis of your findings will most likely involve descriptive text that uses direct quotes, verbatim descriptions, drawings, photographs, and other materials to represent and reinforce major themes. Frequently, evaluation studies utilize both quantitative and qualitative methods, and the presentation and analysis of the data may include both statistical treatments and descriptive text.

Quantitative Data: Summarizing Data in Graphs

The most common way of presenting quantitative data is to plot them on a graph so the patterns in the data can be made apparent visually. The choice of graph depends on the nature of the underlying data. Bar graphs are the simplest way to display data. The vertical, or y axis usually designates the magnitude of the dependent variable, usually a number or a time interval. In figure 18, for example, the vertical axis shows the number of museums established in each decade. The horizontal, or x axis usually represents

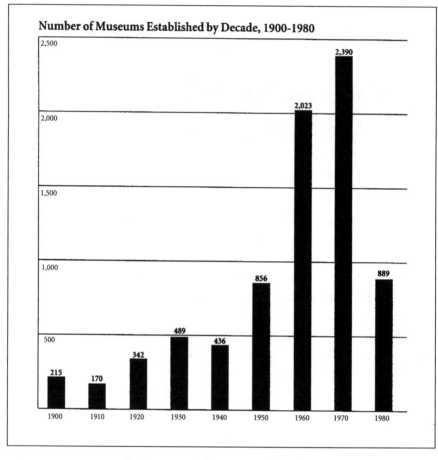

Figure 18. A bar graph of the number of museums established by decade, from 1900 to 1980 (American Association of Museums 1994:35).

the categories of the independent variable, in this case each decade from 1900 to 1980.

If the measurement items require longer descriptions, it is sometimes desirable to reverse the axes. In figure 19, the frequency of occurrence is located on the horizontal axis and the unit of measurement is on the vertical axis.

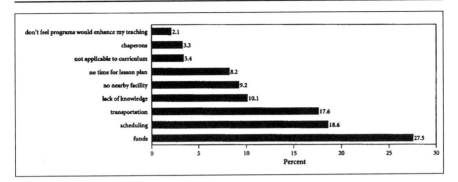

Figure 19. A bar graph (with reversed axes) of the percent of subjects that made various responses to the question, "What are the most serious barriers to increasing your use of nonformal institutions?" A total of 5,691 teachers were surveyed (World Wildlife Fund 1994:18).

Graphs can include the results of statistical tests in various ways. In figure 20, the comparisons that are statistically significant are indicated on the graph.

A bar graph is called a histogram when the categories form a continuous series along a single dimension, and the bar heights represent the number or proportion of observations in each category. Histograms are useful because they display details of the distribution of a variable. For example, figure 21 presents a pattern of use of a tidepool exhibit in which more people stay for shorter times and fewer remain for longer periods.

Histograms are often used to indicate variability in the data, since each bar represents many subjects. In figure 22, the responses to items from a questionnaire are represented in a frequency histogram. The total number of subjects was presented in the legend and the values were expressed as percentages of the total.

Line graphs place single data points to show trends in continuous data. In figure 23, the occurrence of behaviors at exhibits is plotted over the course of an entire museum visit.

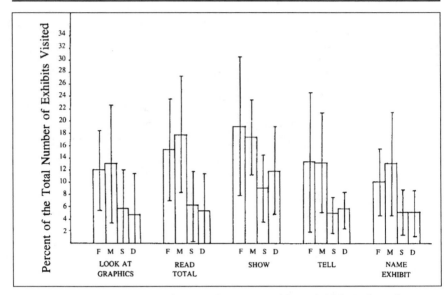

Figure 20. A bar graph showing the mean frequencies and standard deviations of common behaviors by group membership type. This study was based on observations of eighty-one people in twenty-eight family groups that visited the Exploratorium and the Lawrence Hall of Science (Diamond 1986:147). Only behaviors with statistically significant differences are shown (analysis of variance with Newman-Keuls post-hoc comparisons). F = fathers, M = mothers, S = sons, D = daughters. In order to control for length of visit (longer visits would generate more behaviors), frequencies were calculated as the number of times a behavior occurred, divided by the total number of exhibits visited. Each behavior represents a summary category that includes the individual behaviors described in figure 8.

Another kind of graph is called a pie chart. This type can be used only when the data represents parts of a whole, as in the case of percentages (figure 24). Compared to other kinds of graphs and tables, pie charts contain relatively small amounts of data. They also can be difficult to interpret because people generally find it harder to estimate quantities expressed as angles than as distances (Cleveland 1985).

A scatter plot, shown in figure 25, shows another way to illustrate the relationships among variables.

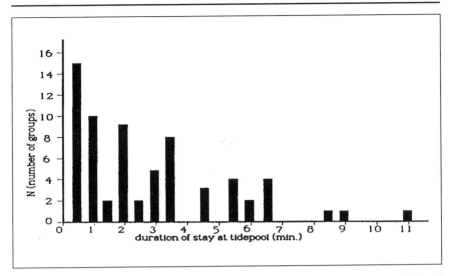

Figure 21. A histogram of the number of visitor groups by duration of stay at a tidepool exhibit at the Steinhart Aquarium at the California Academy of Sciences (Taylor 1986:144).

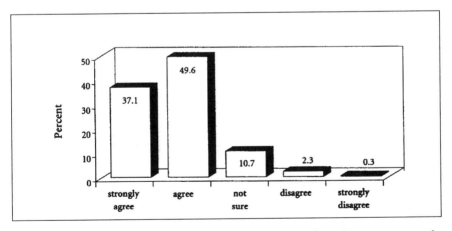

Figure 22. A histogram of the percentage of subjects that made various responses to the question, "Our educational staff understands the concept of biodiversity and related issues." A total of 685 nonformal educators were surveyed (World Wildlife Fund 1994:10).

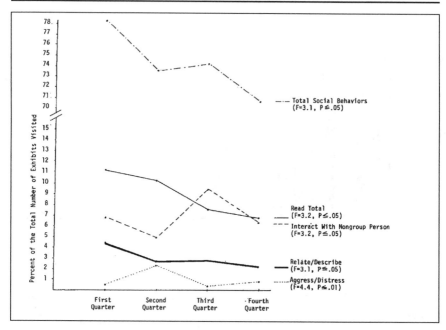

Figure 23. A line graph showing mean frequencies of behaviors over the course of visits of eighty-one people in twenty-eight family groups to the Exploratorium and the Lawrence Hall of Science (Diamond 1986:147). The distributions were compared using analysis of variance; the graph includes only significant changes in the frequencies of behavior over each quarter of the visit.

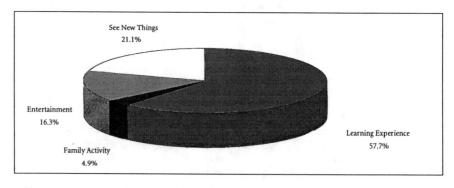

Figure 24. A pie chart showing the responses to the question, "If you visit a museum, what is the one thing you expect to get from that visit?" A total of 1697 ethnically diverse people in the San Francisco Bay Area were interviewed over the phone. Subjects' answers were grouped into the categories on the pie chart (Museum Management Consultants 1994: 31).

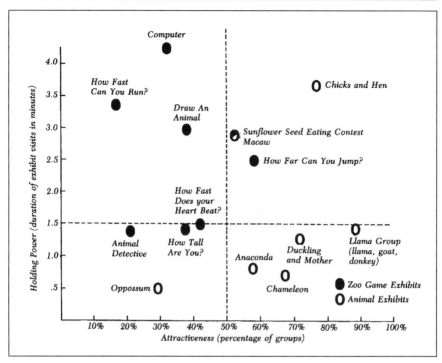

Figure 25. A scatter plot indicating the rating of various zoo exhibits by "holding power" and "attractiveness." Holding power was measured as the mean duration of exhibit visits; attractiveness was measured as the percentage of groups that visited the exhibit. Zoo games tended to have greater holding power, and animal exhibits had greater attractiveness. Data were collected at an experimental mini-zoo at the Lawrence Hall of Science (Rosenfeld 1982:200).

Graphs can be as clear or as confusing as an author chooses. Clear graphs that communicate data well take planning and organization. If a legend is used, it should be clear and concise, including a title, a brief description of the data, and the number of subjects, if applicable. In reports, graphs should be identified by figure number, with the number and legend always placed *beneath* the graph. (Note that the number and legend always go *above* a table.)

Graphs should be understandable without additional information from the text. When you complete a graph, show it to someone who is not familiar with the subject matter. That person should be able to interpret it just on the basis of what is presented in the graph and the legend. According to William Cleveland (1985:100–101), graphing data should be an iterative, experimental process. He suggests some guiding principles:

- Make the data stand out. Use visually prominent graphical statements to show the data so that the interesting features of the graph are obvious. Do not clutter the data region by overdoing the number of data labels, notes, keys, or marks in the data region. Put keys and markers just outside the data region and put notes in the legend or in the text. Keep the graph clear enough for the visual clarity to be preserved under reduction and reproduction.

- The scale of a graph is the ruler along which we graph the data. Choose the scales so that the data fill up as much of the data region as possible. Tick marks indicate the scale like the inch marks on a ruler. Choose the range of tick marks to include or nearly include the range of data, but don't overdo the number of tick marks. Put tick marks outside of the data region. Choose comparable scales when two graphs are to be compared.

- Do not insist that the zero always be included on a scale showing magnitude. If you do use zero, make sure the axis line will not obscure the data points. If this appears to be an issue, move the zero slightly along the axis so the data points will be easy to see.

- Use a scale break (shown on the vertical axis on figure 23) only when necessary. If a break cannot be avoided, place it so that numerical values do not connect on two sides of a break.

Quantitative Data: Summarizing Data in Tables

Tables can be a useful way to summarize data for a report. Tables do not replace graphs, since they rarely can communicate complex patterns and trends in data; but they offer an advantage in that they can include the complete data on a particular topic. According to Edward Tufte (1983), tables are the best way to show exact numerical values, and they are preferable to graphics for many small data sets. They also work well when the data presentation requires many localized comparisons. Nevertheless, in many reports, tables are relegated to appendices or to a background data report; they are not usually included in shorter, summary reports.

There are instances, however, when tables are useful, even essential. When statistical tests have been performed on the data, a table can either provide a condensed summary of the findings (tables 8 and 9) or summarize general

Table 8. A table of the comments of zoo and museum visitors that referred to a knowledge source, gave an opinion, or sought information while they visited the London Zoo or the Natural History Museum in London.

Category	Zoo number n = 459	Zoo %	Museum n = 407	Museum %	Chi-square (1 df)
I know	28	6	80	20	36.31 p<0.001
I think that . . .	140	31	158	39	6.62 p<0.025
Asking a question: "why? what?"	132	29	184	45	25.19 p<0.005
Direction identification "That is a . . ."	191	42	225	55	16.15 p<0.005
Total knowledge source	254	55	296	73	28.15 p<0.005

Source: Tunnicliffe 1996:137.

Table 9. These tables show the responses of former Exploratorium Explainers to the following questions:

> *After you stopped working in the Exploratorium: We'd like to know what ways being an explainer affected your life. To what extent did the Explainer program have an impact on you?* (Circle your response to each).

Fourteen alternatives were given as well as a write-in "other" possibility. The items shown in the tables showed a high degree of association on a subsequent factor analysis. The items listed in the *upper* table showed factor loadings of 0.3 or better on Factor #1, which we designated "Measures of program impact on science and learning." The items listed in the *lower* table showed factor loadings of 0.3 or better on Factor #2, which we designated "Measures of program impact on communication and self-esteem." The percent high impact indicates the percent of subjects who rated a particular item 4 or 5 (the highest ratings). Rated impacts indicated the arithmetic means of all ratings of the item. Further comparisons were also made using analysis of variance. Significant differences among these groups were indicated in the tables.

Measures of Program Impact on Science and Learning		
	Percent High Impact (N=116)	Rated Impact Mean and S.D.
Your curiosity about how things work.	80	4.2 (0.9)
Your interest in science.	67	3.8 (1.2)
Your confidence that you could understand science.	66	3.8 (1.2)
The amount you watch science programs on TV or listen to them on the radio.	35	2.8 (1.4)
The amount you read about science or scientists.	32	3.0 (1.2)
The number of science courses you took or plan to take in school or college.	32	2.9 (1.4)*

*Ratings of students indicating a high interest in science in high school were significantly higher ($p < 0.001$) than for other students.

Measures of Program Impact on Communication and Self-Esteem*		
	Percent High Impact (N=116)	Rated Impact Mean and S.D.
Your ability to teach people.	80	4.2 (0.9)
Your desire to work with people.	73	4.0 (1.0)
Your desire to learn on your own.	63	3.7 (1.1)
Your understanding of your capabilities.	62	3.7 (0.9)
Your self-confidence.	60	3.9 (0.9)
Your effectiveness in other jobs.	50	3.7 (1.1)

*Ratings of female Explainers on factor 2 were significantly higher ($p < 0.03$) than the rating of male Explainers on this factor.

Source: Diamond et al. 1987: 649.

themes (table 10).

Tables that make comparisons are very useful. In table 11, Beverly Serrell (1977) compared what subjects felt their visit was to what it should be.

Like graphs, tables can be useful ways to summarize the results of a questionnaire or interview item (tables 12 and 13).

A table also may summarize a single feature from an observational study (table 14).

Tables require just as careful thought and organization as do graphs. Here are some general guidelines for constructing tables:

- Tables should be listed as "table (number)" and should include a title. The legend, if used, should provide a brief description of the data. Statistical tests performed on the data may or may not be included in the legend. The table number and the legend should be placed at the top of the table.

Table 10. This table summarizes the kinds of sources of information that subjects use when visiting the Steinhart Aquarium at the California Academy of Sciences.

Information from other visitors
- stories of family history
- pointing out familiar animals
- attitudes toward display specimens
- proper behavior in the aquarium

Information from direct observation
- appearance and morphology of display specimens
- brief visual exploration of displays

Information from reading labels
- names of fish
- factual tidbits

Source: Taylor 1986:151.

Table 11. This table categorizes the adjectives used by visitors in their conversations while at the Shedd Aquarium in Chicago.

Adjectives Selected by Visitors to Describe Aquarium Visit*

	Visit Was (%)	Visit Should Be (%)
Informative	49	58
Entertainment	47	45
Educational	47	60
Recreation	34	25
Looking at an exhibit	16	7
Disappointing	1	—

*Totals exceed 100% because of multiple choices.

Source: Serrell 1977:51.

Table 12. This table compares two schools on the types of barriers to teaching hands-on science. This study was part of an evaluation of the School-in-the-Exploratorium program.

Factors Identified at Each School as Major Barriers to the Teaching of Hands-on Science	Meadow School (% of teachers)	Oxnard School (% of teachers)
A lack of science content knowledge	0	20
An aversion to science; tendency to ignore it	7	20
An "overcrowded curriculum"; not enough time to teach science	28	30
A lack of good activities	21	40
A lack of appropriate science materials	14	50
A lack of workable storage/management system for materials	14	50
Not enough pre time to find/set-up materials	35	60
Teaching science is not school/district priority	7	20
A lack of money for materials	7	70
Class size is too large for hands-on science	14	30

Source: St. John et al. 1992:32.

Table 13. A table of where subjects recalled going on field trips as a function of their age.

Where did you go?	Age			
	9–10 yrs. %	13–14 yrs. %	20+ yrs. %	Overall %
Natural history museum	11.8	8.3	13.0	10.9
Zoo or aquaria	5.9	18.8	10.7	12.1
Art museum	0.0	2.1	4.3	2.3
History museum	2.9	4.2	2.2	3.1
Science-technology center	2.9	6.3	17.4	9.4
Nature center/outdoor area	58.0	14.6	17.2	27.1
Other	8.9	14.4	22.2	16.4
Can't remember	0.0	4.2	6.5	3.9
Total	100.0	100.0	100.0	100.0
Number of replies (N)	34	48	46	128

Source: Falk and Dierking 1997:214.

Table 14. Percentage breakdown of the length of stops to the Mankind Discovering Gallery at the Royal Ontario Museum, based on a sample of 100 respondents.

Length of stop	Total stops (%)
Up to 5 seconds	18
6-10 seconds	28
11-30 seconds	31
Over 30 seconds	23

Source: Alt and Griggs 1989:20.

- Refer to the table in the text, so the reader's attention is directed to the table at the appropriate time.

- Don't try to put so much information in a table that it becomes difficult to read. Several shorter, simpler tables are often more desirable than one very complex one.

- Tables should not require more than a few minutes to read and comprehend. The text should be large enough so a magnifying glass won't be required for average readers.

- Remember that the report may be copied. Don't use colors or close shades that could be confused in a black-and-white version.

There are general principles that apply to any kind of data graphic, whether it be a table, a graph, or other form of graphic presentation. Tufte (1983:183) summarizes the elements that make up a "friendly," or easy-to-use, data graphic from one that is difficult to use. Friendly graphics have the following characteristics:

- Words are spelled out; mysterious and elaborate encoding is avoided.

- Words run from left to right, the usual direction for reading occidental languages.

- Little messages help explain the data.

- Elaborately encoded shadings, cross-hatching, and colors are avoided; instead, labels are placed on the graphic itself. No legend is required.

- Graphic attracts viewer, provokes curiosity.

- Colors, if used, are chosen so the color-deficient and color-blind (5 to 10 percent of viewers) can make sense of the graphic (blue can be distinguished from others by most color-deficient people).

- Type is clear, precise, modest; lettering may be done by hand.

- Type is upper-and-lower case, with serifs.

Unfriendly graphics have the following features:

- Abbreviations abound, requiring the viewer to sort through text to decode abbreviations.

- Words run vertically, particularly along the y axis; words run in several different directions.

- Graphic is cryptic, requires repeated references to scattered text.

- Obscure codings require going back and forth between legend and graphic.

- Graphic is repellent, filled with chartjunk.

- Design insensitive to color-deficient viewers; red and green used for essential contrasts.

- Type is clotted, overbearing.

- Type is all capitals, sans serif.

Quantitative Data: Comparing Data Sets

For many purposes, well-constructed graphs or tables will communicate the results of a quantitative analysis, but when you wish to make comparisons between the results of different conditions or to show associations between variables, statistical testing is required. To learn more about the details of data analysis, including the nuts and bolts of statistical computation, you should refer to an introductory statistics text. This section provides a brief overview of the considerations involved in selecting a method of analysis. The first steps are to decide what kinds of data you have and what kinds of questions you want to ask of it.

There are three types of quantitative data that are collected in informal educational studies: counts, measures, and ratios. A count is simply the number of times that something occurred or the number of subjects in a particular category. Examples might be the number of females between twenty and thirty years of age that visited a museum during a particular period or the number of questions asked of a volunteer. Counts are always integers and always greater than or equal to zero.

Measures are variables that result from using a measuring device, such as a yardstick or stopwatch. Distance and time are the most common measures: How far away do visitors stand from an exhibit or from each other? How long do they spend at each exhibit? Unlike counts, measures are continuously distributed, with a level of precision that is limited only by your measuring device.

The third type of data is a ratio. A ratio might represent, for example, the number of times visitors looked at the graphics throughout the course of their visit divided by the total number of exhibits visited. When the ratio is between two counts or two measures of the same type, it is called a proportion or percentage. An example is the percentage of people that answered yes to an interview question. Whether your data is a count, a measure, or a percentage will influence the type of statistical analysis you can use.

Data analysis commonly uses the following terms:

- *Normal distribution, or bell curve*: When the same measurement is taken repeatedly, the values obtained will not all be identical. Because of random factors, successive measurements will differ from each other at least a bit. If the measurements are taken of different subjects, or of the same subject at different times, the variability will be even larger. With enough repetitions, the random factors will average out, producing a distribution that, when graphed, is shaped rather like a bell. The central value of the bell, then, is the best estimate of the value of the variable.

- *Mean*: The most common estimate of the center of a distribution is the mean, or arithmetic average, of the distribution. The values of the variable are added across all observations, and the sum is divided by the number of observations.

- *Standard deviation*: The standard deviation is a measure of how a set of measurements varies from the mean. It is the average deviation of each observation in the distribution from the mean. If your data are normally distributed, one standard deviation on each side of the mean will include 68% of your data. Many calculators and common statistical packages are programmed to calculate the standard deviation for you.

- *Median*: The median is the value of the observation that forms the midpoint of a distribution: Half of the data fall below the median, and half fall above it. Medians are preferable to means as descriptors when the data are not normally distributed.

There are many kinds of statistical tests, and their use depends on the type of data and the questions you plan to ask about the data. Statistical analyses are mainly designed to address three types of questions: questions about distributions, questions about magnitudes, and questions about association.

- *Chi-squared test* is a common technique for comparing distributions. It is particularly valuable for analyzing counts, such as responses to questionnaires or multiple-choice tests. For example, table 8 shows how the chi-squared test can be used to compare each category of visitor comments in a zoo with those in a museum.

- *Analysis of variance, or the student's t-test,* assesses difference in magnitude by comparing means and standard deviations. These tests can be applied to counts, measures, or ratios. If there are only two categories being contrasted, you compare them using the student's t-test; if there are more than two contrasting groups, you use analysis of variance. For example, in figure 23, analysis of variance is used to compare how behavior patterns differ between the first, second, third, and fourth quarters of a visit. In this case the measure of the behaviors was the mean proportion (a ratio) of exhibits where particular behaviors occurred.

- *Correlations address questions of association.* This technique is used to determine the relationship between two different measures or ratios. The straight line that best describes the relationship between the two variables is computed, yielding an estimate of the degree of influence of one variable on the other. This estimate, the correlation coefficient, is equal to one when the two variables rise and fall simultaneously. It is equal to minus one when high levels of one variable are associated with low levels of the other. When there is no meaningful association between variables, the correlation coefficient is zero. From knowledge of the correlation coefficient and the sample size, you can make statements of varying degrees of confidence about the relationship between the variables. As an example, correlation can be used to determine the relationship between the length of time visitors spend at an exhibit and its degree of interactivity.

Qualitative Data

The methods of dealing with qualitative data are more diverse than those dealing with quantitative data, and there are fewer fixed rules. The following categories summarize a few of the common ways to organize qualitative findings (from Patton 1987:147–150):

- *Description*: Sometimes an entire activity will be reported in detail and depth because it represents a typical experience. Descriptions are written in narrative form to provide a holistic picture, and they frequently include photographs, audiotapes, and other kinds of documentation.

- *Case study*: Also written in narrative form, cases can be critical events, communities, people, project sites, or programs.

- *Content analysis*: This method specifies important themes, patterns, and issues in the data. Look for quotations and observations that go together. Read through field notes and organize them under central themes.

- *Inductive analysis*: This method is similar to content analysis, but the themes emerge from the data itself, not from any preconceived themes or issues.

In all of these methods, once the themes have been identified, quotations from study participants are used to provide examples or illustrations of more general principles. Use of quotations is an important element in the analysis and presentation of qualitative research. Quotations can show common patterns in how visitors feel about and interpret their environment. Quotations can also be a powerful tool in demonstrating individual differences, since they emphasize the variability among visitors to informal educational settings.

Quotations can be used in a variety of ways. The question-and-answer form is useful when the interviewer's presence sets a needed context. According to John Brady (1977), the question-and-answer form gives readers precise answers to basic questions about complex issues, and it provides a clear window that allows the subject to speak directly to the reader.

Direct quotations are often the most effective way of conveying a visitor's experience. We obtained the following quotations from a series of in-depth interviews of Explainers working at the Exploratorium in San Francisco (Diamond et al. 1987:647). Explainers are high-school-aged students from very diverse backgrounds who are paid to help visitors use the exhibits. We asked them to talk about how the museum program influenced them:

> I grew. I grew up here. I had a lot of prejudiced views. I was raised in a traditional Chinese family that has a prejudice against blacks. There was one person here I was particularly attached to. She broke down a lot of deep barriers. She taught me everyone has a veneer, and to break through that veneer is to take each person as a soul.
>
> *Wilson, Explainer in 1979.*

I used to tolerate a lot of my own mistakes. On the floor you fall on your face a lot in front of those that know better. Once at an eye dissection, I got into a conversation with an ophthalmology student. I'd be explaining things but all of a sudden I was learning new stuff by talking to this guy.

Gabe, Explainer in 1981.

Indirect quotations can also be effective, as shown in the following description by Michael Spock:

The anecdote that I think is perhaps most exciting is the one in which Steven Jay Gould talks about his first visit to the American Museum in New York. It wasn't just the Yankees that imprinted him, but it was the Tyrannosaurus that he saw on his first visit. He talks about that as a pivotal point in his life. He says that at age five or six, when he first saw the Tyrannosaurus, he knew that he was going to do something for the rest of his life related to that experience. It made a difference to Gould; it got him going and thinking about dinosaurs and then paleontology and then evolution; and evolution was the thing he ended up studying. I also think that the drama of this event has something to do with the fact that Gould has a deep commitment to popularization, for which he gets a lot of criticism from his colleagues. (1988: 257)

Paulette McManus has recorded many visitor conversations in museums, and she often uses direct quotations within her papers. The following examples show two different ways that she uses direct quotations to illustrate a point:

Visitors sometimes talked back to the "museum someone" who was communicating with them. In another transcript, the visitor reads aloud: "Are you a primate? Yes, you are a primate," Then he answers out loud, "No, I'm not." (McManus 1989a:5)

If visitors are asked in an authoritarian manner to
interact physically at a hands-on exhibit and can't
quite see the purpose, they will respond very
negatively:
  Is that a totally meaningless game?
  I must say that's totally barmy. I can't quite see
the hell of it. (McManus 1989b:185)

Robert Wolf and Barbara Tymitz (1978:24) give useful
guidelines for writing up the results of qualitative evaluations, including participant observation. They suggest two
steps. The first is a phase of data-expansion questions that
reseachers should ask themselves to elaborate on the findings. Some examples of data-expansion questions are:

- What are the possible explanations for (a) the observed
  situation, (b) the stated emotion or feeling, (c) the
  confusion, (d) the problem? Your inferences and
  explanations may refer to historical factors, specific
  observations you made, statements written in collected
  documents, collected responses in agreement or
  disagreement, and your thoughtful intuitions.

- What solutions are offered to phenomenon x?

- What are the barriers to solutions of phenomenon x?

A second phase in the analysis of qualitative data involves data reduction—selecting and condensing the data
to a manageable form that can be summarized in a report.
Qualitative studies often produce huge volumes of data that
need considerable synthesis if they are to be understood by
clients. Wolf and Tymitz (1978:25) suggest the following
data reduction questions:

- What factors, or situations seem to be related?

- Do they stem from the same source, cause, or feeling?

- Is there a word that can be used to describe a number of related factors?

- What are the kinds of relationships between and among a number of phenomena?

- Is there a phrase that could identify the above-diagrammed relationship (e.g., the relationship of the larger label and hands-on opportunity to visitor reaction)?

Chapter 8

Preparing an Evaluation Report

Writing an Evaluation Report for Publication

Evaluation reports are often written for a particular client, but all too often these studies end up in someone's drawer rather than where other researchers can read them. A client that funds a study has the prerogative of deciding whether that report can be made public. Many people, however, recognize that evaluation reports have value to the entire informal education research community, and that each report helps further the work of the whole field. Therefore, it is often desirable to publish evaluation reports in recognized journals (figure 26) and to present the findings at conferences.

Many published reports use some variation based on a scientific report format. The basic format is as follows:

- Abstract
- Introduction
- Methods
- Results
- Conclusions
- Bibliography

The abstract is a very brief description of the entire research or evaluation project. In one paragraph, you will need

Art Education

Curator

European Journal of Science Education

History News

ILVS Review

The International Journal of Museum Management and Curatorship

International Journal of Science Education

Journal of Biological Education

Journal of Aesthetic Education

Journal of Museum Education

Journal of Research in Science Teaching

Museum News

National Art Education Association Studies in Art Education

Physics Today

The Public Garden

Science and Children

Science Education

Visitor Behavior

Figure 26. Some of the journals that accept and publish submitted manuscripts on museum, zoo, aquarium, and botanic garden evaluation studies.

to state the purpose of the study, the methods used, the primary results, and the importance of the findings. The abstract should be a brief, but clear overview of the entire study so that readers can quickly determine its relevance to their own interests.

The introduction includes a statement of the purpose of the study, a brief description or history of the institution or exhibit being studied, and a review of previous work that has some bearing on the purpose, methods, or results.

The literature review may summarize previous work conducted at the same institution or similar ones, or it may describe studies that used similar methodologies or that influenced the choice of methodology used in your study. Most importantly, the literature review should summarize what is already known about the problem or issue you are investigating. For example, if you plan to study the behavior of families in a zoo, you should describe the previous work in this area.

Literature reviews in informal education can often be difficult, because the literature is scattered in many different places. Evaluation studies may be found in journals in the fields of art, humanities, education, science education, museums, and sometimes science. In addition, many evaluations are not published in journals, but are distributed as reports among individual museums. This means that a literature review requires a substantial effort in digging for sources. In spite of the effort required, a literature review is an essential part of an evaluation report. It shows that you are aware of previous work in your area and that you have made every effort to build upon what has already been learned.

The methods section should summarize your data-gathering techniques in some detail. Describe whom your subjects were, how many there were, and how they were sampled. Explain how you collected your data: for example, if you interviewed your subjects, how many questions were asked, how long did the interviews last, and how did you code the responses? If you conducted observations, what categories of behaviors did you use, and how did you establish them? If you used a questionnaire, how many questions were asked, where did subjects fill it out, and how was it returned? Essentially, the presentation of the methods should be in enough detail to allow another researcher to replicate your study.

Sometimes it is useful to include in the methods section a more detailed description of the setting for your study. For example, if you were collecting tracings of visitors' movements throughout a museum, it could be helpful to provide a map of the galleries with a brief overview of their contents. This helps the reader to visualize the setting for your study and can make the results much easier to understand.

The results section is where the findings of your study are presented. How the findings are organized may be crucial to their usefulness. Your results may include both qualitative and quantitative information. For instance, if you gathered detailed information on a sample, you may be able to say something about the demographics of visitors even if the primary purpose of your study was not to survey the audience. Be sure to examine all aspects of your data and ask what information would be useful to your readers. Next, consider how the data should be organized. Often, the best way to present interview or questionnaire results is not in the order that questions were asked. They are ordered in the interview to make them easy for the subjects to respond to and to reduce biases. For a report, however, they should be arranged to make them comprehensible to the reader and to emphasize critical findings. Preferably, group the findings into similar headings or themes and present them in order of their relative importance.

It is usually helpful to present quantitative information in graphs or tables, so that patterns are easy to recognize. The text of the results section should describe the major findings, even if they are also presented in a graph or other figure or in a table. The text should indicate the figure or table for the reader. Qualitative parts of your study are usually presented in a series of descriptions in the text. When you have a great amount of detailed information to present, you may choose to provide a separate section in which to describe each major theme. Graphics, photographs, or diagrams can also be very useful in summarizing both qualitative and quantitative information.

The conclusions should state what is important about your results. Don't just restate the results, but rather describe how your findings are relevant to your intended readers. Did your data support the results of previous work in this area? Did it contradict some other work? Did it raise some new issues that have not been discussed before? Evaluation studies in museums, zoos, and parks are often quite exploratory, and the results of one study can often raise more questions than they answer. This can be very useful for deciding what direction to take in future research. In the conclusions, you should examine the big picture: what is happening in your study site and what your results imply for similar situations.

Often an evaluation study is problem-centered, and the readers want to know what solutions you can offer. Your client may want to know, for example, why so few visitors enter a particular gallery. Your results may describe where visitors actually go, and how they made decisions about their movements. In the conclusions, you should present your best notions, based on your findings, of why the visitors chose one gallery over another. It is fair to be speculative, as long as you base your conclusions on the data you have presented in the report.

The bibliography is the last section, and it includes the bibliographic references that you cite in your report. Journals normally have published submission procedures that will give you their preferred style for listing references.

The format of a publishable paper is sometimes not the most helpful document for the client of an evaluation report. Even when you plan to publish the evaluation study, it can be useful to write the report first in a format that directly meets your client's needs. Administrators, board members, and sometimes members of the press may not want to spend the time digging through a lengthy and detailed report.

It is often useful, therefore, to create a brief summary report that is accompanied by the more complete record of the evaluation. The summary report should usually be no more than five pages, about the length or your initial evaluation proposal. It should clearly state the purpose of the study, how the data were collected, what the major findings were, and the conclusions. The detailed information and data can be put into the more lengthy background report to answer questions about details.

Less often, clients may request other kinds of documentation of the study. A video summary may be requested, or a photo-journal. Visual formats can be very effective ways to convey the results of an evaluation study to clients. Make sure that you establish the desired format for the report with the client at the beginning. Then you can prepare the necessary documentation throughout the course of your study.

You may find it useful to have access to resources on how to write clearly for a wide audience. The references listed in the bibliographies in this book contain useful guidelines on form, style, grammar, and many other helpful suggestions for writing well. The *Publication Manual of the American Psychological Association* (1994) and *The Chicago Manual of Style* (1993) also give advice on such items as citing references in the text, notes, abbreviations, capitalization, guidelines for nonsexist language, and the proper format for graphs, tables, and bibliographies.

Afterword

Evaluation is less about data collection than it is about immersion. It is about becoming so familiar with an institution, exhibit or program that it becomes second nature. Whether the data you collect is qualitative, quantitative, or a combination of the two, it will be your own intuitive understanding of the opportunities and limitations of the informal culture that will be a primary guide for your study. Robert Stake cautions that accumulating large data sets isn't enough:

> The key mistake, I think, is the assumption that objective information can be aggregated across large numbers of students or visitors to provide a basis for decision-making to people who are not personally acquainted with the program. The key hope, I think, is that subjective information based on key issues, oriented to real problems and particular situations, rigorously cross-examined, will become a standard offering of evaluation studies. (Smithsonian Institution 1979:16)

Everyone who has ever worked in a museum, zoo, or botanical garden is an expert to some degree on how visitors experience their institution. And yet the findings of an evaluation report may still be surprising. We should wonder at the depth of some people's experiences, particularly when we expected them to be superficial. We should consider how quickly some children run through a museum, when we expected them to stop and look closely. We should remark at how long some visitors spend at the exhibits, and how short a time others do. And we should marvel when someone remembers back and knows exactly what the zoo animals did, which dinosaurs were on display, and what flowers were in bloom, when they first visited an institution an entire lifetime ago.

References Cited

Ackerman, Edith K.
   1988 Pathways into a child's mind: Helping children become epistemologists.
   In *Science learning in the informal setting: Symposium proceedings*, edited
   by P. G. Heltne and L. A. Marquardt. Chicago: Chicago Academy of
   Sciences.

Alt, Michael B., and Steven Griggs
   1989 *Evaluating the Mankind Discovering Gallery.* Toronto: Royal Ontario
   Museum.

American Association of Museums
   1994 *Museums count.* Washington, D.C.: American Association of Museums.

American Psychological Association
   1994 *Publication manual of the American Psychological Association.* Fourth
   Edition. Washington, D.C.: American Psychological Association.

Andrews, Kathryne
   1979 Teenagers' attitudes about art museums. *Curator* 22(3): 224–32.

Brady, John
   1977 *The craft of interviewing.* New York: Random House.

Brooks, Joyce A. M., and Philip E. Vernon
   1956 A study of children's interests and comprehension at a science museum.
   British Journal of Psychology 47:175–82.

The Chicago manual of style
  1993   Chicago: University of Chicago Press.

Cleveland, William S.
  1985 *The elements of graphing data*. Monterey, Calif.: Wadsworth Advanced
         Books and Software.

Department of Health, Education, and Welfare
  1979 *The Belmont Report. Ethical principles and guidelines for the protection of
         human subjects of research*. Washington, D.C.: U.S. Government Printing
         Office.

Diamond, Judy
  1980 *The ethology of teaching: A perspective from the observations of families in
         science centers*. Ph.D. diss., University of California, Berkeley.
  1982 Ethology in museums: Understanding the learning process. *Roundtable
         Reports* 7(4): 13–5.
  1986 The behavior of family groups in science museums. *Curator* 29(2):
         139–54.
  1996 Playing and learning. *ASTC Newsletter* 24(4): 2–6.

Diamond, Judy, Alan Bond, Beth Schenker, Debra Meier, and Dana Twersky
  1995 Collaborative multimedia. *Curator* 38(3): 137–49.

Diamond, Judy, Anita Smith, and Alan Bond
  1988 California Academy of Sciences Discovery Room. *Curator* 31(3):
         157–66.

Diamond, Judy, Mark St. John, Beth Cleary, and Darlene Librero
  1987 The Exploratorium's Explainer Program: The long-term impacts on
         teenagers of teaching science to the public. *Science Education* 71(5):
         643–56.

Dienes, Zoltán, and Dianne Berry
  1997 Implicit learning: Below the subjective threshold. *Psychonomic Bulletin
         and Review* 4(1): 3–23.

Dierking, Lynn D.
  1987 *Parent-child interactions in a free choice learning setting: An examination
         of attention-directing behaviors*. Ph.D. diss., University of Florida.

Falk, John H.
    1983 Time and behavior as predictors of learning. *Science Education* 67(2): 267–76.

Falk, John H., and Lynn D. Dierking
    1992 *The museum experience.* Washington, D.C.: Whalesback Books.
    1997 School field trips: Assessing their long-term impact. *Curator* 40(3): 211–18.

Feher, Elsa
    1990 Interactive museum exhibits as tools for learning: Explorations with light. *International Journal of Science Education 12(1): 35–49.*

Feher, Elsa, and Karen Rice
    1985 Development of scientific concepts through the use of interactive exhibits in a museum. *Curator* 28(1): 35–46.

Feher, Elsa, and Karen Rice Meyer
    1992 Children's conceptions of color. *Journal of Research in Science Teaching.* 29(5): 505–20.

Fischer, Daryl K.
    1997 Visitor Panels: In-house evaluation of exhibit interpretation. In *Visitor studies: Theory, research and practice*, Vol. 9, edited by Marcella Willis and Ross Loomis. Jacksonville, Fl.: Visitor Studies Association.

Gallistel, Charles R.
    1990 *The Organization of Learning.* Cambridge: MIT Press.

Gordon, Beverly
    1995 "They don't wear wigs here": Issues and complexities in the development of an exhibition. *American Quarterly* 47(1): 116–39.

Griggs, Steven A.
    1983 Orienting visitors within a thematic display. *The International Journal of Museum Management and Curatorship* 2:119–34.

Griggs, Steven A., and Jane Manning
    1983 The predictive validity of formative evaluation of exhibits. *Museum Studies Journal* 1(1): 31–41.

Hazlett, Brian A., ed.
   1977 *Quantitative methods in the study of animal behavior.* New York:
        Academic Press.

Hilke, D. D.
   1989 The family as a learning system: An observational study of families in
        museums. In *Museum visits and activities for family life enrichment,*
        edited by Barbara H. Butler and Marvin B. Sussman. New York:
        Haworth Press.

Hilke, D. D., and John D. Balling
   1985 The family as a learning system: An observational study of family
        behavior in an information rich environment. In *The role of the family in
        the promotion of science literacy,* edited by D. D. Hilke and John D.
        Balling. Washington, D.C.: National Science Foundation.

Hilke, D. D., Elizabeth C. Hennings, and Myriam Springual
   1988 The impact of interactive computer software on visitors' experiences: A
        case study. *International Laboratory for Visitor Studies Review* 1(1):
        34–49.

Hofstein, Avi, and Sherman Rosenfeld
   1996 Bridging the gap between formal and informal science learning. *Studies
        in Science Education* 28:87–112.

Klein, Marty
   1981 Recall versus recognition. In *Activities handbook for the teaching of
        psychology,* edited by Ludy T. Benjamin, Jr. and Kathleen D. Lowman.
        Washington, D.C.: American Psychological Association.

Larkin, Jill
   1989 Display-based problem solving. In *21st century Carnegie-Mellon
        symposium on cognition, complex information processing: The impact of
        Herbert A. Simon,* edited by D. Klahr and K. Kotovsky. Hillsdale, N.J.:
        Lawrence Erlbaum.

Larkin, Jill, and Barbara Rainard
   1984 A research methodology for studying how people think. *Journal of
        Research in Science Teaching* 21(3): 235–54.

Lazlo, Ervin, Robert Artigiani, Allan Combs, and Vilmos Csányi
   1996 *Changing visions, human cognitive maps: Past, present, and future.*
       Westport, Conn.: Praeger.

Loomis, Ross J.
   1973 Please not another visitor survey. *Museum News* 52(2): 21–6.
   1974 Social learning potentials of museums. Talk given at symposium, The
       Museum as a Learning Environment, American Educational Research
       Association, 16 April 1974, Chicago.

Lorenz, Konrad Z.
   1950 The comparative method in studying innate behavior patterns.
       Symposia of the Society for Experimental Biology 4:221–68.

Martin, Paul, and Patrick Bateson
   1988 *Measuring behaviour.* Cambridge, England: Cambridge University
       Press.

McCreedy, Dale
   1997 Survey for the program, Girls at the Center. Philadelphia: Franklin
       Institute Science Museum.

McManus, Paulette M.
   1989a What research says about learning in science museums: Watch your
       language! People do read labels. *ASTC Newsletter* 17(3): 5–6.
   1989b Oh Yes, they do: How museum visitors read labels and interact with
       exhibit texts. *Curator* 32(3): 174–89.
   1991 Toward understanding the needs of museum visitors. In *The manual of
       museum planning,* edited by G.D. Lord and B. Lord. London: H.M.S.O.

Melton, Arthur W.
   1933 *Problems of installation in museums of art.* Washington, D.C.: American
       Association of Museums.
   1935 Studies of installation at the Pennsylvania Museum of Art. *Museum
       News* 12:5–8.

Miles, Roger S., M. B. Alt, D. C. Gosling, B. N. Lewis, and A. F. Tout
   1988 *The design of educational exhibits.* London: Unwin Hyman.

Museum Management Consultants, Inc., and Polaris Research and Development
  1994 *Bay Area research project: A multicultural audience study for Bay Area museums.* Vols. 1 and 2. San Francisco: Bay Area Research Project Consortium.

Nahemow, Lucille.
  1971 Research in a novel environment. *Environment and Behavior* 3(1): 81–102.

National Science Foundation
  1998 *Elementary, secondary, and informal education program announcement and guidelines.* Washington, D.C.: National Science Foundation.

Nicholson, Heather Johnston, Faedra Lazar Weiss, and Patricia Campbell
  1994 Evaluation in informal science education: Community-based programs. In *Informal learning: What the research says about television, science museums, and community-based projects,* edited by Valerie Crane. Dedham, Mass.: Research Communications Ltd.

Norman, Donald A.
  1982 *Learning and memory.* New York: W. H. Freeman and Company.

Oppenheimer, Frank
  1972 The Exploratorium: A playful museum combines perception and art in science education. *American Journal of Physics* 40:978–84.
  1980 Adult play. *Exploratorium Magazine* 3(6): 1–3.
  1986 *Working prototypes.* San Francisco: Exploratorium.

Oppenheimer, Frank, and Karen C. Cole
  1974 The Exploratorium: A participatory museum. *Prospects* 4(1): 1–10.

Patton, Michael Quinn
  1987 *How to use qualitative methods in evaluation.* Newbury Park, Calif.: Sage Publications.

Piaget, Jean
  1973 *To understand is to invent: The future of education.* New York: Penguin Books.

Piaget, Jean, and Bärbel Inhelder
  1969 *The psychology of the child.* New York: Basic Books.

Pick, Herbert L., Jr.
    1993 Organization of spatial knowledge in children. In *Spatial representation*,
        edited by N. Eilan, R. McCarthy, and B. Brewer. Oxford: Blackwell.

Reif, Fredrick, and Jill H. Larkin
    1991 Cognition in scientific and everyday domains: Comparison and
        learning implications. *Journal of Research in Science Teaching* 28(9):
        733–760.

Rice, Karen, and Elsa Feher
    1987. Pinholes and images: Children's conceptions of light and vision. *Science
        Education* 71(4): 629-639.

Robinson, Edward S.
    1931 Exit the typical museum visitor. *Journal of Adult Education* 3(4):
        418–423.

Robinson, Edward S., Irene C. Sherman, and Lois E. Curry
    1928 *The behaviour of museum visitors*. n.s. 5. Washington, D.C.: American
        Association of Museums.

Roschelle, Jeremy
    1995 Learning in interactive environments: Prior knowledge and new
        experience. In *Public institutions for personal learning*, edited by John H.
        Falk and Lynn D. Dierking. Washington, D.C.: American Association of
        Museums.

Rosenfeld, Sherman
    1982 A naturalistic study of visitors at an interactive mini-zoo. *Curator* 25(3):
        187–212.

Salant, Priscilla, and Don A. Dillman
    1994 *How to conduct your own survey*. New York: John Wiley and Sons.

Serrell, Beverly
    1977 Survey of visitor attitude and awareness at an aquarium. *Curator* 20(1):
        48–52.
    1997 Paying attention: The duration and allocation of visitors' time in
        museum exhibitions. *Curator* 40(2): 108–125.

Shettel, Harris
    1993 Professional standards for the practice of visitor research and evaluation
        in museums. *Musuem News* 72(5): 63–66.

Smithsonian Institution
    1979 *An abstract of the proceedings of the Museum Evaluation Conference,* June
        23–24, 1977. Washington, D.C.: Smithsonian Institution Office of
        Museum Programs.

Spiegel, Amy N., and Teresa Dethlefs
    1997 *Evaluation of the Wonderwise Project.* Lincoln, Neb.: University of
        Nebraska State Museum.

Spock, Michael
    1988 What's going on here: Exploring some of the more elusive, subtle signs
        of science learning. In *Science learning in the informal setting: Symposium
        proceedings,* edited by P. G. Heltne and L. A. Marquardt. Chicago:
        Chicago Academy of Sciences.

St. John, Mark
    1987a *Evaluation design: The evaluator and the architect.* Evaluation Guides
        12. Portland: Northwest Regional Educational Laboratory
    1987b *Evaluation design: Selecting methods.* Evaluation Guides 14. Portland:
        Northwest Regional Educational Laboratory.

St. John, Mark, Barbara Heenan, and Becky McClaskey
    1992 *An assessment of the school in the Exploratorium program 1988–1991.*
        Inverness, Calif.: Inverness Research Associates.

Taylor, David
    1991 Evaluating prototypes. In *Try it! Improving exhibits through formative
        evaluation,* edited by Samuel Taylor. Washington, D.C.: Association of
        Science-Technology Centers.

Taylor, Samuel
    1986 *Understanding processes of informal education: A naturalistic study of
        visitors to a public aquarium.* Ph.D. diss., University of California,
        Berkeley.

Taylor, Samuel, ed.
    1991 Evaluation techniques. In *Try it! Improving exhibits through formative evaluation*, edited by Samuel Taylor. Washington, D.C.: Association of Science-Technology Centers.

Tufte, Edward R.
    1983 *The visual display of quantitative information*. Cheshire, Conn.: Graphics Press.

Tunnicliffe, Sue Dale
    1996 Conversations within primary school parties visiting animal specimens in a museum and zoo. *Journal of Biological Education* 30(2): 130–41.

Twersky, Dana
    1994 *Mesozoic gallery evaluation: Summary of notes and reports*. Lincoln: University of Nebraska State Museum.

Tye, Michael
    1993 Image indeterminacy: The picture theory of images and the bifurcation of 'what' and 'where' information in higher level vision. In *Spatial representation*, edited by N. Eilan, R. McCarthy, and B. Brewer. Oxford: Blackwell.

University of Nebraska-Lincoln Institutional Review Board
    1997 *University of Nebraska-Lincoln Institutional Review Board guidelines for the protection of human subjects in research studies*. August. Lincoln: University of Nebraska.

Wiegman, Paul G., and Pamela M. Wiegman
    1973 *The Smithsonian grasshopper, a research report*. Washington, D. C.: Smithsonian Institution.

Wolf, Robert L., and Barbara L. Tymitz
    1978 *A preliminary guide for conducting naturalistic evaluation in studying museum environments*. Washington, D.C.: Smithsonian Office of Museum Programs.

World Wildlife Fund
    1994 Windows on the wild, Results of a national biodiversity survey. Washington, D.C.: World Wildlife Fund.

Other Publications
of Interest

American Association of Museums
    1997 *A strictly informal survey: Professional education needs for college/ university museums and galleries.* Washington, D.C.: American Association of Museums.

Anderson, Scarvia B.
    1968 Noseprints on glass or how do we evaluate museum programs? In *Museums and education,* edited by E. Larrabee. Washington, D.C.: Smithsonian Institution Press.

Bicknell, Sandra, and Graham Farmelo
    1993 *Museum visitor studies in the 90s.* London: Science Museum.

Birney, Barbara
    1986 *A comparative study of children's perceptions and knowledge of wildlife and conservation as they relate to field trip experiences at the Los Angeles County Museum of Natural History and the Los Angeles Zoo.* Ph.D. diss., University of California at Los Angeles.

Bitgood, Stephen, Beverly Serrell, and Don Thompson
    1994 The impact of informal education on visitors to museums. In *Informal learning: What the research says about television, science museums, and community-based projects,* edited by Valerie Crane. Dedham, Mass.: Research Communications.

Borun, Minda
    1993 Naive knowledge and the design of science museum exhibits. *Curator* 36(3): 201–19.

Borun, Minda, Margaret Chambers, and Ann Cleghorn
    1996 Families are learning in science museums. *Curator* 39(2): 123–38.

Borun, Minda, and Jennifer Dritsas
    1997 Developing family-friendly exhibits. *Curator* 40(3): 178–96.

Borun, Minda, Margaret Chambers, Jennifer Dritsas, and Julie I. Johnson
    1997 Enhancing family learning through exhibits. *Curator* 40(4): 279–95.

Butler, Barbara H., and Marvin B. Sussman, eds.
    1989 *Museum visits and activities for family life enrichment*. New York:
        Haworth Press.

Cohen, Dorothy H., and Virginia Stern
    1958 *Observing and recording the behavior of young children*. New York:
        Teachers College Press.

Crane, Valerie
    1994 Understanding the dynamics of informal learning. In *Informal learning:
        What the research says about television, science museums, and community-
        based projects*, edited by Valerie Crane. Dedham, Mass.: Research
        Communications.

Csikszentmihalyi, Mihály, and Kim Hermanson
    1995 Intrinsic motivation in museums: Why does one want to learn? In
        Public Institutions for Personal Learning, edited by John H. Falk and Lynn
        D. Dierking. Washington, D.C.: American Association of Museums.

Derwin, Claudia W., and Joan B. Piper
    1988 The African Rock Kopje exhibit evaluation and interpretive elements.
        Environment and Behavior 20(4): 435–51.

Diamond, Judy
    1991 Prototyping interactive exhibits on rocks and minerals. *Curator* 34(1):
        5–17.
    1992 New directions for research. In *Patterns in practice*, edited by S. Nichols.
        Washington, D.C.: Museum Education Roundtable.
    1994 Sex differences in science museums: A review. *Curator* 37(1): 17–24.

Diamond, Judy, and Alan Bond
    1983 The transmission of learned behavior: an observational study of father-
    child interactions during fishing. *Ethology and Sociobiology.* 4:95–110.

Dierking, Lynn D., and John H. Falk
    1994 Family behavior and learning in informal science settings: A review of
    the research. *Science Education* 78(1): 57–72.

Dierking, Lynn D., and Wendy Pollock
    1998 *Questioning assumptions: An introduction to front-end studies in
    museums.* Washington, D.C.: Association of Science and Technology
    Centers.

Dixon, Beverly R., Gary D. Bouma, and G. B. J. Atkinson
    1987 *A handbook of social science research methods.* Oxford: Oxford
    University Press.

Doering, Zehava D., Andrew J. Pekarik, and Audrey E. Kindlon
    1997 Exhibitions and expectations: The case of "Degenerate Art." *Curator*
    40(2): 126–42.

Douglas, Jack
    1985 *Creative interviewing.* Beverly Hills: Sage Publications.

Falk, John H.
    1991 Analysis of the behavior of family visitors in natural history museums:
    The National Museum of Natural History. *Curator* 34(1): 44–50.
    1993 *Leisure decisions influencing African American use of museums.*
    Washington, D.C.: American Association of Museums.

Falk, John H., and Lynn D. Dierking, eds.
    1995 *Public institutions for personal learning.* Washington, D.C.: American
    Association of Museums.

Falk, John H., John J. Koran, Lynn D. Dierking and L. Dreblow
    1985 Predicting visitor behavior. *Curator* 28:249–57.

Flagg, Barbara N.
    1990 *Formative evaluation for educational technologies.* Hillsdale, N.J.:
    Lawrence Erlbaum Associates.

Gennaro, Eugene D.
  1981 The effectiveness of using previsit instructional materials on learning
        for a museum field trip experience. *Journal of Research in Science
        Teaching* 18(3): 275–9.

Ginsberg, Herbert, and Sylvia Opper
  1969 *Piaget's theory of intellectual development, An introduction.* Englewood
        Cliffs, N.J.: Prentice-Hall.

Gottfried, Jeffry
  1979 *A naturalistic study of children's behavior in a free-choice learning
        environment.* Ph.D. diss., University of California at Berkeley.
  1980 Do children learn on school field trips? *Curator* 23(3): 165–74.

Griggs, Steven A.
  1981 Formative evaluation of exhibits at the British Museum (Natural
        History). *Curator* 24(3): 189–201.

Gurian, Elaine H.
  1995 A blurring of the boundaries. *Curator* 38(1): 31–7.

Hein, Hilde
  1990 *The Exploratorium: The museum as laboratory.* Washington, D.C.:
        Smithsonian Institution Press.

Hood, Marilyn G., and Lisa C. Roberts
  1994 Neither too young nor too old: A comparison of visitor characteristics.
        Curator 37(1): 36–45.

Hooper-Greenhill, Eilean
  1994 *Museums and their visitors.* London and New York: Routledge.

Jarrett, Joanna E.
  1986 Learning from developmental testing of exhibits. *Curator* 29(4):
        295–306.

Koran, John J. Jr., and Jim Ellis
  1991 Research in informal settings: some reflections on designs and
        methodology. International Laboratory of Visitor Studies Review 2(1):
        67–86.

Koran, John J. Jr., Mary Lou Koran, and Sarah J. Longino
1986 The relationship of age, sex, attention, and holding power with two types of science exhibits. *Curator* 29(3): 227–35.

Koran, John J. Jr., Sarah J. Longino, and Lynn D. Shafer
1983 A framework for conceptualizing research in natural history museums and science centers. *Journal of Research in Science Teaching* 20(4): 325–39.

Koran, John J. Jr., Laura Morrison, Jeffrey R. Lehman, Mary Lou Koran, and Luisa Gandara.
1984 Attention and curiosity in museums. *Journal of Research in Science Teaching* 21(4): 357–63.

Korn, Randi
1995 An analysis of differences between visitors at natural history museums and science centers. *Curator* 38(3): 150–60.

Kubota, Carole A., and Roger G. Olstad
1991 Effects of novelty-reducing preparation on exploratory behavior and cognitive learning in a science museum setting. *Journal of Research in Science Teaching* 28(3): 225–34.

Lave, Jean
1988 *Cognition in practice.* Cambridge: Cambridge University Press.

Lehman, Jeffrey R.
1986 Docent questioning behavior during tours with elementary school children. *Curator* 29(4): 259–63.

Loftus, Elizabeth F., Bjorn Levidow, and Sally Duensing
1992 Who remembers best? Individual differences in memory for events that occurred in a science museum. *Applied Cognitive Psychology* 6:93–107.

Loomis, Ross J.
1987 *Museum visitor evaluation: New tool for management.* Nashville: American Association for State and Local History.

Lucas, A. M., and Paulette McManus
1986 Investigating learning from informal sources: Listening to conversations and observing play in science museums. *European Journal of Science Education* 8(4): 342–52.

McManus, Paulette M.
    1987 It's the company you keep . . . The social determination of learning-
        related behaviour in a science museum. *International Journal of Museum
        Management and Curatorship* 6:263–70.
    1988a Good companions: More on the social determination of learning-
        related behaviour in a science museum. *The International Journal of
        Museum Management and Curatorship* 7:37–44.
    1988b Do you get my meaning? Perception, ambiguity and the museum
        visitor. *International Laboratory of Visitor Studies Review* 1(1): 62–75.

Merrill, Jenefer
    1975 *Documentation of exhibits. The Exploratorium, December 1974–June
        1975.* San Francisco: Exploratorium.

Nahemow, Lucille
    1971 Research in a novel environment. *Environment and Behavior* 3(1):
        81–102.

Neubacher, Donald L.
    1983 *Preferences for selected interpretive exhibits.* M.S. thesis, Humboldt State
        University, Arcata, Calif.

Nichols, Susan K.
    1990 *Visitor's surveys: A user's manual.* Washington, D.C.: American
        Association of Museums.

Pekarik, Andrew J.
    1997 Understanding visitor comments: The case of *Flight Time Barbie.*
        Curator 40(1): 56–68.

Ramey-Gassert, Linda, Herbert J. Walberg III, and Herbert J. Walberg
    1994 Reexamining connections: Museums as science learning environments.
        Science Education 78(4): 345–63.

Rosenfeld, Sherman
    1980 *Informal learning in zoos: Naturalistic studies of family groups.* Ph.D.
        diss., University of California, Berkeley.

Sachatello-Sawyer, Bonnie
    1996 *The status of adult education methodology in museums.* Ph.D. diss.,
        Montana State University.

Sackett, Gene P., ed.
>   1978 *Observing behavior. Vol. II: Data collection and analysis methods.*
>   Baltimore: University Park Press.

Screven, Chandler
>   1991 What is formative evaluation? In *Try it! Improving exhibits through
>   formative evaluation*, edited by Samuel Taylor. Washington, D.C.:
>   Association of Science and Technology Centers.

Semper, Robert J.
>   1990 Science museums as environments for learning. *Physics Today* 43(11):
>   50–6.

Serrell, Beverly, ed.
>   1990 *What research says about learning in science museums*, Vol. 1.
>   Washington, D.C.: Association of Science and Technology Centers.
>   1993 *What research says about learning in science museums*, Vol. 2.
>   Washington, D.C.: Association of Science and Technology Centers.

Smithsonian Institution Office of Museum Programs
>   1992 *The audience in exhibit development.* Washington, D.C.: American
>   Association of Museums.

St. John, Mark
>   1990 *First hand learning: Teacher education in science museums.* Washington,
>   D.C.: Association of Science and Technology Centers.
>   1992 Evaluating visitors' conversations with exhibits. In *Patterns in practice*,
>   edited by S. Nichols. Washington, D.C.: Museum Education Roundtable.
>   1993 The Turing Test as an evaluation method. In *Science education
>   partnerships, Manual for scientists and K-12 teachers*, edited by Art
>   Sussman. San Francisco: University of California, San Francisco.

Stronck, David R.
>   1983 The comparative effects of different museum tours on children's
>   attitudes and learning. *Journal of Research in Science Teaching* 20(4):
>   283–90.

Tressel, George W.
>   1980 The role of museums in science education. *Science Education* 64(2):
>   257–60.

Tufte, Edward R.
  1990 *Envisioning Information*. Cheshire, Conn.: Graphics Press.

Vukelich, Ronald
  1984 Time language for interpreting history collections to children. *Museum Studies Journal* 1(4): 43–50.

Williams, Patterson B.
  1974 Find out who Donny is. *Museum News* 52:42–5.
  1975 Perception games and body language: The Philadelphia Museum of Art museum games. *Art Teacher* 5:4–6.

Wolcott, Harry F.
  1995 *The art of fieldwork*. Walnut Creek, Calif.: AltaMira Press.

Figure and Table Credits

FIGURE 3, page 54, "Orienting visitors within a thematic display" by Steven A. Griggs, *Museum Management and Curatorship,* 1983 Volume 2, pps.119–134. Reprinted with permission from Elsevier Science. FIGURE 13, page 103, "Session Evaluation Form: 1994 AAM Annual Meeting." Reprinted with permission. Copyright ©1994, the American Association of Museums. All rights reserved. FIGURE 14, page 107, copyright ©1996 Amy N. Spiegel. Used by permission. FIGURE 15, page 110, reprinted by permission. Copyright ©1987, The Exploratorium, San Francisco. FIGURE 18, page 134, "A histogram of the number of museums established by decade, from 1900 to 1980." Reprinted, with permission, from *Museums Count.* Copyright ©1994, the American Association of Museums. All rights reserved. FIGURE 19, page 135, reprinted with permission from *Windows on the Wild, Results of a National Biodiversity Survey* published by World Wildlife Fund, copyright ©1994. FIGURE 21, page 137, used with permission of Samuel M. Taylor. FIGURE 22, page 137, reprinted with permission from *Windows on the Wild, Results of a National Biodiversity Survey* published by World Wildlife Fund, copyright©1994. FIGURE 24, page 138, illustration used with permission from Adrienne Horn, Museum Management Consultants, Inc., San Francisco, California.

TABLE 2, page 42, *How to Conduct Your Own Survey* by Priscilla Salant & John A. Dillman. Copyright ©1994, John Wiley & Sons. Reprinted by permission of John Wiley & Sons, Inc. TABLE 6, page 98, illustration used with permission from Adrienne Horn, Museum Management Consultants, Inc., San Francisco, California. TABLE 7, page 125, "Children's Conceptions of Color" by Elsa Feher & Karen Rice Meyer, *Journal of Research in Science Teaching,* 1992. Reprinted by permission of John Wiley & Sons, Inc. TABLE 8, page 141, "Conversations within primary school parties visiting animal specimens in a museum and zoo" by Sue Dale Tunnicliffe, *Journal of Biological Education,* 1996. Used by permission of *Journal of Biological Education.* TABLE 9, page 142, "The Exploratorium's Explainer Program: the long-term impacts on teenagers of teaching science to the public" by Judy Diamond, Mark St. John, Beth Cleary, and Darlene Librero, *Science Education,* 1987. Reprinted by permission of John Wiley & Sons, Inc. TABLE 14, page 145, reprinted courtesy of Royal Ontario Museum.

Index

Index of Authors Cited

About the Author

Judy Diamond is a professor at the University of Nebraska State Museum in Lincoln. A biologist and science educator specializing in informal learning, she received her Ph.D. degree from the SESAME Program at the University of California at Berkeley.

Professor Diamond began her museum career at the Exploratorium in San Francisco and the Lawrence Hall of Science at the University of California, Berkeley. At the Exploratorium, she was the evaluator for projects funded by the Rockefeller and the W. K. Kellogg Foundations. Prior to her appointment at the University of Nebraska State Museum, she was deputy director for public programs at the San Diego Natural History Museum.

The author of over forty publications in the fields of museums, science education, and animal behavior, Diamond is the director of the Wonderwise Project, which has created an award-winning, nationally distributed series of science kits based on the work of women scientists. She is co-author, with Alan Bond, of the 1999 University of California Press book *Kea, Parrot of Paradox: The Evolution and Behavior of a New Zealand Parrot.*

A member of the editorial board of *Curator* magazine, Judy Diamond has served on the boards of directors of the American Association of Museums, the Friends of the Earth, and the Earth Island Institute. She has served on advisory panels for the Howard Hughes Medical Institute, the National Institutes of Health, and the Stanford Research Institute, and has been an advisor for more than twenty museums in the United States and Israel.

About the Cover Artist

This book's cover art is from "Human Connections," a work created by Austine Wood Comarow for the Boston Museum of Science in 1987 with a grant from the Polaroid Corporation. The imagery depicts the history of communication from petroglyphs to space travel. The original work, which is twenty-five by twenty-seven feet, uses a technique called Polage, in which layers of clear cellulose are sandwiched between two polarizing filters.

Austine was born in Kentucky and raised in Geneva. She developed the concept of Polage in 1967 and had her first major show in the Museo de Belles Artes in Santiago, Chile, in 1973. Her large-scale works may be seen in public institutions in the United States, France, Japan, Singapore, and Switzerland. Her website is http://www.austine.com.